D1572137

DEMCO

LEADING INDICATORS FOR THE 1990s

LEADING INDICATORS FOR THE 1990s

Geoffrey H. Moore
Center for International Business Cycle Research
Graduate School of Business
Columbia University

Dow Jones-Irwin
Homewood, Illinois 60430

This publication is designed to provide accurate and authoritative information in regard to the subject matter covered. It is sold with the understanding that neither the author nor the publisher is engaged in rendering legal, accounting, or other professional service. If legal advice or other expert assistance is required, the services of a competent professional person should be sought.

From a Declaration of Principles jointly adopted by a Committee of the American Bar Association and a Committee of Publishers.

Project editor: Jane Lightell
Production manager: Ann Cassady
Jacket design: Mike Finkelman
Compositor: Spectrum Publisher Services, Inc.
Typeface: 11/13 Times Roman
Printer: R. R. Donnelley & Sons Company

Library of Congress Cataloging-in-Publication Data

Moore, Geoffrey Hoyt.
    Leading indicators for the 1990s / Geoffrey H. Moore.
        p.   cm.
    Includes index.
    ISBN 1-55623-258-6
    1. Economic indicators—United States. I. Title.
HC106.8M66   1990   89–34886
    330.973—dc20   CIP

Printed in the United States of America
1 2 3 4 5 6 7 8 9 0 D O 6 5 4 3 2 1 0 9

CONTENTS

CHAPTER 1

AN OVERVIEW

Geoffrey H. Moore

The primary objectives of this study have been to reevaluate the Commerce Department's leading, coincident, and lagging indicators; develop and test new indicators; and make the indicator system more representative of the present-day economy. The work began in March 1986 with the support of a grant to the Center for International Business Cycle Research by the Alfred P. Sloan Foundation and supplementary support from the Department of Commerce. A number of scholars affiliated with the Center have participated, including Charlotte Boschan, John Cullity, Lorene Hiris, Philip Klein, Allan Layton, and Victor Zarnowitz. We benefited also from the guidance of an Advisory Committee, chaired by Edgar R. Fiedler of the Conference Board.[1]

This chapter summarizes our recommendations regarding the content of the composite indexes published in *Business Conditions Digest* (BCD). We then offer some suggestions for additional indicators, including a leading index for the service industries and a leading index of export demand. Chapters 2 to 17 describe the new indicators developed for various economic sectors.

After the study was completed, the Commerce Department in March 1989 issued a revised set of leading, coincident, and lagging indicators, adopting some of our recommendations. We have not revised our report to reflect these changes, but comment on them at the end of this chapter.

---

[1]The other committee members are: Phillip Cagan, Columbia University; Robert J. Gordon, Northwestern University; Saul H. Hymans, University of Michigan; Allen Sinai, Boston Co. Economic Advisors; and Allan H. Young, Bureau of Economic Analysis.

PROPOSED CHANGES IN BCD LEADING INDEX

We are proposing to increase the number of leading indicators from 11 to 15 and to compile both a long-leading and a short-leading index. We recommend retaining some series from the present list, substituting several series for similar series in the present list, and adding series not now represented (see Table 1-1). One of the objectives met by the new list is to include only series that are available for the preceding month at the time the index is first released, thus avoiding a major cause of revisions in the existing index. Brief notes concerning the new indicators as well as the replacements follow. The new list of 15 indicators has been classified into a long-leading and a short-leading group, with indexes constructed for each group. The long-leading index has led business cycle turns by 11 months, on average, and has led both the short-leading index and the BCD leading index by about 6 months (see Chart 1-1). In addition, at the end of this section, we propose the development of leading and coincident indexes that would be more promptly available than the BCD indexes.

TABLE 1-1
Changes in the List of Leading Indicators

BCD List (prior to 1989)	CIBCR Recommended Lists	
	Short-Leading	Long-Leading
	New Indicators	
	Index of net change in business population	Index of bond prices, Dow Jones
	Layoff rate	Ratio, price to unit labor cost, manufacturing
	Replacements	
New housing permits, index	—	New housing permits, number
Change in manufacturing and trade inventories, in 1982 $	Inventory change survey, National Association of Purchasing Management	

TABLE 1-1—*Continued*

BCD List (prior to 1989)	CIBCR Recommended Lists	
	Short-Leading	*Long-Leading*
Vendor performance, Chicago Purchasing Management Association	Vendor performance, National Association of Purchasing Management	
Change in sensitive materials prices	Industrial materials prices, growth rate, *Journal of Commerce*	
Change in business and consumer credit outstanding	Domestic nonfinancial debt, in constant $, growth rate	
	Unchanged	
Money supply (M2), in 1982 $	—	Money supply (M2), in 1982 $
Average workweek, manufacturing	Average workweek, manufacturing	
Initial claims, unemployment insurance	Initial claims, unemployment insurance	
New orders, consumer goods and materials, in 1982 $	New orders, consumer goods and materials, in 1982 $	
Contracts and orders, plant and equipment, in 1982 $	Contracts and orders, plant and equipment, in 1982 $	
Stock price index, S&P 500	Stock price index, S&P 500	

Abbreviations: CIBCR, Center for International Business Cycle Research; BCD, *Business Conditions Digest.*

1. The Commerce Department's index of net business formation (BCD series 12) was dropped from the leading index in March 1987. This action conformed to one of our early recommendations, but we have since developed a new measure based on business starts and business failures and suggest that it be included in the leading index (see Chapter 2). The starting up of new business enterprises plays an important role in a free

CHART 1–1
Three Leading Indexes

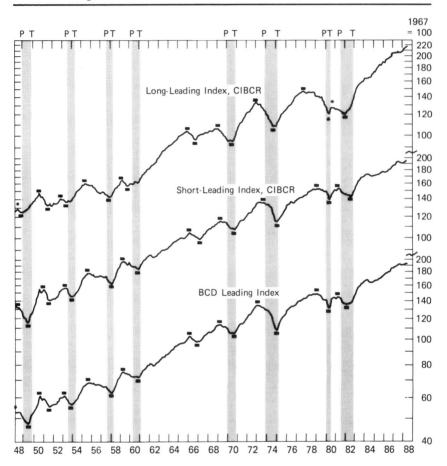

Shaded areas are business cycle recessions, from peak (P) to trough (T). BCD, *Business Conditions Digest.*

Source: Center for International Business Cycle Research (CIBCR), August 1988.

enterprise economy and has been especially significant in the service sector. Data used in our index are available weekly from Dun & Brad-street Corp.

  2. A new layoff rate series has been constructed from data in the Bureau of Labor Statistics (BLS) household survey of employment and unemployment. The new series is a good leading indicator, is available promptly, and supplements initial claims for unemployment insurance

(BCD series 5), because it is not directly affected by changes in unemployment insurance regulations, funding, or coverage (see Chapter 3).

3. Since bond prices move inversely with bond yields, an index of bond prices provides a way to look at the inverse effect of changes in long-term interest rates on the economy. We find that bond prices lead the business cycle by very long intervals, but are closely associated with other leading indicators, such as building permits and stock prices. The inclusion of the bond price index will help remedy one of the deficiencies of the leading index, namely, very short leads at business cycle troughs (see Chapter 4).

4. The availability of a new BLS net output price index for manufacturing, which eliminates intraindustry sales, makes it feasible to construct a monthly price/cost ratio that is a good proxy for profit margins. Heretofore only quarterly series have been available. The addition of a profit margin indicator to the leading index will be an important conceptual improvement because of the influence such margins have on investment commitments (see Chapter 5). Our study has also revealed the need to improve the existing lagging indicator, unit labor cost in manufacturing (BCD series 62) (see Chapter 14).

5. Current monthly data on the change in manufacturing and trade inventories (BCD series 36) are not available when the leading index is compiled. Since the series often moves sharply, its inclusion a month later produces a substantial revision in the index. The National Association of Purchasing Management (NAPM) survey of inventory change is available promptly, and its record as a leading indicator is similar to that of BCD series 36 (see Chapter 6). Hence, we recommend that the NAPM series be used to represent this variable in the leading index.

6. The NAPM survey of vendor performance provides national coverage for this measure of delivery times. We propose that it be used in place of the corresponding series from the Chicago Purchasing Management Association (BCD series 32). For a comparison of the two series and an analysis of their relation to the ratio of inventories to sales, see Chapter 6.

7. The six-month smoothed growth rate in the new *Journal of Commerce* index of industrial materials prices should, we believe, be substituted for the smoothed change in sensitive materials prices (BCD series 99). The new index was designed by the Center for International Business Cycle Research (CIBCR) and has been published daily since September 1986. The 18 commodities included constitute a more comprehensive and up-to-date list of important materials than other indexes of this type. Also, the new index avoids the duplication involved in BCD series 99, which combines two indexes with overlapping coverage (see Chapter 7).

8. Because the existing series on the change in business and consumer debt in current dollars (BCD series 111) is no longer a good leading indicator at troughs, we have explored a number of alternatives. The best one seems to be the six-month smoothed growth rate in total debt in 1982 dollars. The new series is a comprehensive measure of real purchasing power provided by the credit system and leads at both peaks and troughs. Although final estimates of this series for the current month are presently not available when the leading index is released, we hope that the Federal Reserve Board (FRB) and the Commerce Department will recognize the importance of providing a preliminary estimate for this purpose (see Chapter 8). If this cannot be done, we recommend that the debt series be dropped as a component of the leading index, because all the other recommended series are available by the index release date.

9. A minor change in the list of indicators would be substituting the number of new housing permits for the presently used index of housing permits (BCD series 29). The two series are essentially identical, but the numbers are widely referred to in the press, which means that they are readily understood by the public, and can easily be updated by users of the indicators.

10. With the 15 recommended indicators it becomes feasible to construct two composite indexes, one based on 4 indicators with especially long leads, the other with 11 short leaders. The long-leading index not only permits a farther glimpse ahead, but also helps to interpret the subsequent movements in the short-leading index. Growth rates in the long-leading index obtained from data available in September appear capable of producing acceptable forecasts of real gross national product (GNP) growth for the year ahead (see Chapter 9).

11. We have also given consideration to the construction of more promptly available leading and coincident indexes, using indicators that are published either daily or weekly or at least very early in the following month. This would advance the publication date of the indexes by about three weeks. A list of 12 leading indicators and 3 coincident indicators that meet this criterion has been developed, and composite indexes have been constructed and tested (see Chapter 10).

PROPOSED CHANGES IN BCD
COINCIDENT INDEX

1. Substitute total nonfarm employee-hours for nonfarm employment (BCD series 41). Aggregate hours is a better measure of labor input than number employed, especially with a growing number of persons employed part-time in service industry jobs. This series is currently published in BCD (series 48), but is not used in the index. Two deficiencies in the series should be removed: avoid a publication lag by using an estimating procedure developed by CIBCR, and eliminate occasional erratic movements by adjusting the average workweek for holidays that occur in the survey week. The latter improvement is being undertaken by the BLS and will also improve one of the leading indicators, the average workweek in manufacturing (BCD series 1). For further discussion, see Chapter 12.

2. Substitute retail sales and capital goods sales in constant dollars for manufacturing and trade sales in constant dollars. The latter has several deficiencies. One is that it is not available when the coincident index is released, so that the preliminary coincident index is based on only three indicators and is revised the following month. Another is that sales of goods are overweighted as compared with services, because the same goods may be sold by manufacturers to wholesalers and by wholesalers to retailers. If a monthly approximation to real final sales could be obtained, it would implicitly give more weight to services. We have experimented with several alternatives and recommend that an aggregate of retail sales and capital goods sales, in constant dollars, be used to replace manufacturing and trade sales (see Chapter 11).

3. Develop a monthly index of total passenger and freight traffic. This would be one way of giving better representation of the service industries in the coincident index, because transportation is an important service sector and is more sensitive to business cycles than many other service industries. The FRB has developed such an index on an experimental basis, back to 1977. This should be evaluated and, if possible, extended to earlier years. We might undertake a research project in this field, because we have already developed an index of domestic air traffic and have access to other data (see Chapter 13).

4. Consider developing two types of coincident indexes—one based on the most comprehensive measures of economic activity available monthly, the other based on aggregates that are more cycle sensitive. The new experimental index of goods and services production developed by the FRB belongs in the first group, for example, whereas the industrial production index belongs in the second one. For further illustrations and discussion of this concept, see Chapter 12.

PROPOSED CHANGES IN BCD LAGGING INDEX

1. Substitute the six-month smoothed growth rate in an improved measure of unit labor cost in manufacturing for trend-adjusted unit labor cost (BCD series 62). The improved measure, developed by CIBCR, makes the monthly series consistent with the quarterly figures published by the BLS, which are based on net output originating in manufacturing (see Chapter 14). The use of growth rates avoids the problem of continuously updating the trend that, until it was recently corrected, led to a serious downward bias in BCD series 62.

2. Include the six-month smoothed growth rate in the consumer price index (CPI) of services. This is an important component of the CPI, is a consistent lagging indicator, and will expand the coverage of services in the lagging group. For further discussion, see Chapter 13.

ADDITIONAL INDICATORS AND
FURTHER RESEARCH

Our investigation recognizes that there are many valuable economic indicators that are not readily classified as leading, coincident, or lagging or do not qualify for the indexes in other respects. We have not been able to undertake a complete review of this area, but present some ideas and recommendations below.

A New Index of Unemployment Severity

We have developed a new measure of unemployment severity that takes into account both the number unemployed and the length of time they have been unemployed. Because it usually turns up before a business cycle peak, but does not turn down until after a business cycle trough, it cannot be classified unambiguously as leading or lagging. Nevertheless, the index should provide a useful warning that a recession is beginning and confirmation that it is ending. In addition, it measures the severity of a recession's impact upon workers and the reduction in the burden of unemployment as an expansion proceeds (see Chapter 15).

Service Industry Indicators

There is broad agreement that the economic indicator system should provide better statistical coverage of the rapidly expanding service industries. Some of the recommendations outlined above take steps in that direction, but to treat the subject adequately, we believe a new approach is required. In a separate study supported by the Coalition of Service Industries, we have developed a set of leading and coincident services indicators and composite indexes, analyzed in terms of their growth rates. In this form the services indicators show clear cyclical movements closely related to business cycles. But the indicators in the BCD indexes largely reflect levels of activity, and when the services indicators are expressed in that form, they show almost continuous growth with virtually no cyclical swings. Rather than transform all the BCD indicators into growth rates or mix growth rates in services with levels in other activities, we propose separate treatment (see Chapter 13).

Unemployment Rates for Goods-Producing and Services-Producing Industries

The BLS has, at our request, constructed an unemployment rate for persons previously employed in the service industries comparable with an unemployment rate for the goods-producing industries. We find that both rates move up and down with the business cycle, but that the rate for the goods industries reaches much higher levels in recessions than the rate for the service industries. The risk of unemployment is lower in the latter group. We recommend that these two rates, which, like the total unemployment rate, lead at business cycle peaks and lag at troughs, be presented in BCD (see Chapter 13).

International Indicators

Several pages of the Commerce Department's monthly report on indicators, *Business Conditions Digest,* are devoted to international economic affairs. This is an area of growing importance because foreign trade and investment and the associated prices, interest rates, and exchange rates now play a much larger role in our economy. We have therefore reviewed the indicators of U.S. international transactions and international comparisons and recommend extensive changes, including the introduction of a leading index of U.S. export demand (see Chapter 16).

Inflation Indicators

Although BCD now includes a number of measures of inflation in the section "Prices, Wages, and Productivity," as well as elsewhere, we believe it would be desirable to focus more attention on this area. A number of measures of inflation that are not now in BCD could be presented, including the producer price index for finished goods, the personal consumption expenditures deflator, the gross domestic purchases deflator, import and export price indexes, and the employment cost index. Moreover, series pertaining to inflation might well be brought together in a single section, even though they may also appear in other sections. For example, the survey of expected selling prices by manufacturers, wholesalers, and retailers is now included under "Diffusion Indexes," but the figures are highly relevant to the outlook for inflation. The same is true of the measures of sensitive prices, unit labor costs, and profits. Various leading indicators of inflation might be introduced, following the lines developed by CIBCR. Indeed, given sufficient emphasis and supportive research, leading, coincident, and lagging indicators of inflation might come to be as widely used in the 1990s as business cycle indicators are today.

Diffusion Indexes

BCD contains a section "Diffusion Indexes," which measures how widespread are the expansions or contractions within different groups of indicators. Our impression is that they are seldom used, perhaps because such a large number of indexes are presented, and many of them are erratic. We would propose to drop the erratic one-month span indexes, place the others in the terminal month of the span rather than in the central month, and consolidate five of the indexes based upon leading indicators into one index, covering a nine-month span. This diffusion index that we have constructed covers 164 leading indicators broken down by industry and (in one instance) by state. Because it tells what percentage of this large group of indicators has been rising over the previous nine months, it effectively supplements the information provided by the BCD leading index. It could be released at the same time as the leading index and hence focus attention on a frequently overlooked dimension of business cycles—their scope. This dimension itself has leading characteristics.

Surveys of Economic Forecasts

Surveys reporting the consensus of economists' forecasts are now among the more widely used economic indicators. Some, like *Blue Chip Economic Indicators* and *Worldscan,* are reported monthly. Others, such as the American Statistical Association and National Bureau of Economic Research *(ASA-NBER Survey),* are quarterly, whereas still others, including the *Livingston Survey,* are annual or semiannual. They pertain to future periods ranging from one quarter ahead to a year or more and cover production, unemployment, prices, interest rates, and so on. Many tests of their accuracy have been conducted, with results that generally attest to their usefulness (see Chapter 9 for one example). We recommend, therefore, that a section of BCD be devoted to these surveys, showing current and historical data and measures of accuracy. The development of such a section would be a substantial undertaking, but worthwhile because of the perspective and guidance it would give users of this information.

Scoring of Indicators

The method of scoring leading, coincident, and lagging indicators that has previously been used in their selection and weighting was developed in the 1966 review of the indicators and was used, with various modifications, in the 1975 review. It takes into account economic significance, statistical adequacy, consistency of timing and conformity to business cycles, smoothness, and currency. We have not applied the method systematically to every indicator discussed in this report, partly because we believe some further modifications in the procedure should be made. In particular, it would be desirable to include the results of modern time series analysis procedures in the scoring plan. Further research and testing will be needed to produce an improved scoring system.

THE MARCH 1989 REVISION OF
THE BCD INDEXES

The new leading index issued by the Commerce Department in March 1989 includes 11 indicators, of which 9 are the same as or nearly equivalent to those in our recommended list of 15. The two remaining indicators in the new BCD list are different from any in our list, while six of the indicators in our list are not represented in the new BCD list (see Table 1-2).

Of the two indicators in the BCD index that are not in ours, the change in unfilled orders for durable goods partly duplicates two series that are in both lists, namely, new orders for consumer goods and materials and contracts and orders for plant and equipment. The change in

TABLE 1-2
The New BCD List and the CIBCR List of Leading Indicators

New BCD List (1989)	CIBCR Recommended Lists	
	Short-Leading	Long-Leading
Only in BCD List		
Changes in manufactur-ers' unfilled orders, durable goods, in 1982 $		
Index of consumer ex-pectations		
Only in CIBCR List		
	Index of net change in business population	Index of bond prices, Dow Jones
	Layoff rate	Ratio, price to unit labor cost, manufacturing
	Inventory change sur-vey, NAPM	
	Domestic nonfinancial debt, in constant $, growth rate	

TABLE 1-2—*Continued*

New BCD List (1989)	CIBCR Recommended Lists	
	Short-Leading	Long-Leading
	Same in Both Lists	
Money supply (M2), in 1982 $		Money supply (M2), in 1982 $
Average workweek, manufacturing	Average workweek, manufacturing	
Initial claims, unemployment insurance	Initial claims, unemployment insurance	
New orders, consumer goods and materials, in 1982 $	New orders, consumer goods and materials, in 1982 $	
Contracts and orders, plant and equipment, in 1982 $	Contracts and orders, plant and equipment, in 1982 $	
Stock price index, S&P 500	Stock price index, S&P 500	
Vendor performance, NAPM	Vendor performance, NAPM	
	Close Equivalents in Both Lists	
New housing permits, index		New housing permits, number
Change in sensitive materials prices, smoothed	Industrial materials prices, growth rate, *Journal of Commerce*	

Abbreviations: NAPM, National Association of Purchasing Management; BCD, *Business Conditions Digest;* CIBCR, Center for International Business Cycle Research.

unfilled orders is equal to new orders minus shipments, and orders for durable goods include both consumer goods and machinery. We see no reason for duplicating the orders figures in this way or for including shipments, inversely, in a leading index, especially because they are already included, positively, in the coincident index (in manufacturing and trade sales). The objective, according to the Commerce Department, was to obtain a more promptly available substitute for inventory change. In the CIBCR list this is achieved by using the inventory change survey compiled by the NAPM (see Chapter 6).

The second series in the BCD list that is not in ours is the consumer expectations index from the survey conducted by the University of Michigan. We did not examine this index in the study reported here, but we have done so in a subsequent study. We find that the expectations index, as well as the similar one published by the Conference Board, derives its leading characteristics chiefly from the fact that it reflects changes rather than the level of activity. The questions asked in the survey refer mostly to expected changes, and the results compare closely with the growth rates in coincident indicators of business activity. They also compare closely with diffusion indexes of production and employment. Although such rates of change and diffusion indexes do tend to lead business cycle turns, which represent peaks and troughs in the level of activity, the leading indicators and the composite leading index are not intended to derive their leading characteristics from this fact. In BCD, for example, diffusion indexes and rates of change are placed in a separate section of the publication, as noted above. One reason for excluding them from the leading index is that rates of change decline when the economy slows down, as in 1984–85. An index that includes a diffusion index will be less likely to distinguish recessions from slowdowns.

As for the other leading indicators in our list but not in the new BCD list, the reader may simply refer to the relevant chapters in this book, where their record is presented (Chapters 2–6 and 8). With regard to the lagging indicators, two of our recommendations were adopted in the revised BCD lagging index. They are to include the rate of change in labor costs per unit of output in manufacturing and the rate of change in consumer prices for services (see Chapters 13 and 14). Further representation of service industries in the indicator system, where we have advocated the use of growth rates, should remain on the agenda.

CHAPTER 2

A NEW INDEX OF NET BUSINESS FORMATION

Geoffrey H. Moore

Fluctuation in the creation and discontinuance of business enterprises is a phenomenon of long standing in the history of business cycles. The number of new incorporations and the liabilities of business failures were included in one of the first lists of leading indicators, constructed in 1950. At that time they already had a long record of leading the turns in the business cycle, and they have continued to perform in substantially the same fashion since then.[1] Measures of business formation have been included in the Commerce Department's leading index since its inception. Recently, however, the existing series (BCD series 12) has suffered from two deficiencies. The new incorporations component is no longer compiled promptly because of delays in reporting by state agencies, and the component based upon new business telephones installed is no longer reported on a comprehensive basis. For these reasons the Commerce Department dropped the index of net business formation from the leading index in March 1987, although it has continued to publish the series separately in BCD.

In order not to lose this kind of information, which bears on the vitality of the economy, the confidence of businessmen, and new opportunities for employment or the lack thereof, CIBCR has constructed a

---

[1]See *Recession-Recovery Watch,* CIBCR, June 1986.

new index. It will be available weekly and, hence, promptly enough for use in weekly or monthly leading indexes. It has a long and consistent record of leading business cycle turning points.

The new index has two components, both supplied by Dun & Bradstreet Corporation. One is the newly established series on the number of new business starts, the other is the long-established series on the number of business failures. Since business failures do not cover all types of discontinuances and hence are not fully commensurate with business starts, we do not simply subtract one series from the other. Rather, we treat each as a component of a composite index, with changes in failures taken inversely. The Commerce Department's method of index construction is used except that no adjustment is made in the long-run trend of the index.

CHART 2–1
Two Indexes of Net Business Formation

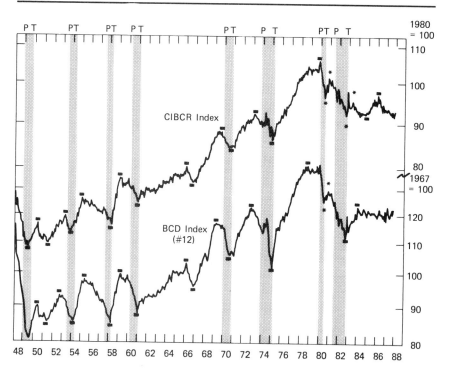

Shaded areas are business cycle recessions, from peak (P) to trough (T). CIBCR, Center for International Business Cycle Research; BCD, *Business Conditions Digest.*

TABLE 2-1
Leads and Lags of Two Indexes of Net Business Formation

Business Cycle		BCD Index (Series 12)		CIBCR Index*	
Peak	Trough	Peak	Trough	Peak	Trough
11/48		−10**		−10**	
	10/49		−3		−4
7/53		−10		−2	
	5/54		−2		−5
8/57		−26		−30	
	4/58		0		0
4/60		−12		−13	
	2/61		−1		−1
12/69		−8		−2	
	11/70		−3		−1
11/73		−11		−8	
	3/75		−1		−2
1/80		−15		−2	
	7/80		−1		−1
7/81		−7		−8	
	11/82		−1		−2

Median					
Peaks and troughs		−10	−1	−8	−2
All turns			−5		−2
Mean					
Peaks and troughs		−12	−2	−9	−2
All turns			−7		−6
Standard deviation					
Peaks and troughs		6	1	9	2
All turns			7		7
Percentage leads					
Peaks and troughs		100	88	100	88
All turns			94		94
Extra cycles (dates)		6/50	5/51	6/50	7/51
		3/66	12/66	2/66	9/66
				1/86	

*Based on number of new incorporations (business starts since 1985) and number of business failures (treated invertedly).
**Index begins in January 1948, so peak may have been earlier.

Because the business starts series begins only in 1985, we have linked new incorporations to it before then. Both components are seasonally adjusted, although it is too early to tell whether we have obtained an adequate adjustment of the three-year series on business starts. The business failures series also has had a change in coverage, beginning in 1984. At that time Dun & Bradstreet developed a new system for reporting failures, which included many more small firms in the service sector. To allow for this we have treated the figures since January 1984 as a separate segment, with an overlap in that month.

The composite index of net business formation constructed from these series is shown in Chart 2-1, together with the previous series (BCD series 12). Their leads and lags at business cycle turns are recorded in Table 2-1. The new index is more erratic in its monthly movement, but its lead/lag record is similar. The new index led at all but 1 of the 16 business cycle peaks and troughs covered, although the leads at troughs were typically short. The average lead was two months at troughs and eight months at peaks. Two extra downswings that did not match business recessions occurred in 1950–51 and 1966–67. These corresponded with slowdowns in the economy, or growth recessions.

Because the new index will be available promptly, we recommend it to replace the previous index of net business formation in the Commerce Department's leading index. By providing a direct count of the births and deaths of service enterprises as well as goods-producing enterprises, it improves the coverage of the leading index in the service sector. We also recommend the new index for inclusion in the formerly published subgroup index, capital investment commitments (BCD series 914), together with new orders and contracts for plant and equipment (BCD series 20) and new housing permits (BCD series 29). This is a very important category among the leading indicators, and it is urgent that this subindex be restored.

CHAPTER 3

A NEW LAYOFF RATE SERIES

Geoffrey H. Moore and John P. Cullity

Layoff rates have long been used as a leading indicator in business cycle analysis. The layoff rate in manufacturing was initially selected as a leading indicator in 1960, and appeared in the first issue of *Business Conditions Digest* (then called *Business Cycle Developments*) in 1961. It continuously appeared in BCD until the labor turnover survey of manufacturing establishments was discontinued by the BLS for budgetary reasons at the end of 1981. The Commerce Department then replaced it with initial claims for unemployment insurance as a component of the leading index.

We have found that a layoff rate with characteristics very similar to those of the discontinued series can be obtained from the number of job losers on layoff reported by the BLS from its household survey. These persons are classified by the length of time they have been unemployed. The shortest time class covers those who had been laid off within the past five weeks and are still unemployed. This group obviously corresponds closely to those previously included in reports by employers on the number of employees laid off in the past month. It has more comprehensive coverage than manufacturing and can be converted to a layoff rate by dividing by total civilian employment. The result is a new leading indicator, available since 1969 when the BLS began reporting the number of unemployed classified by reason for unemployment (Charts 3-1 and 3-2).[1]

---

[1]The new series was first described in G. H. Moore and J. P. Cullity, "A New Leading Indicator: Workers Recently Laid Off," *Monthly Labor Review*, May 1986, pp. 35–37.

CHART 3-1

Layoff Rates: Manufacturing, 1948–81; Total under Five Weeks, 1969–85

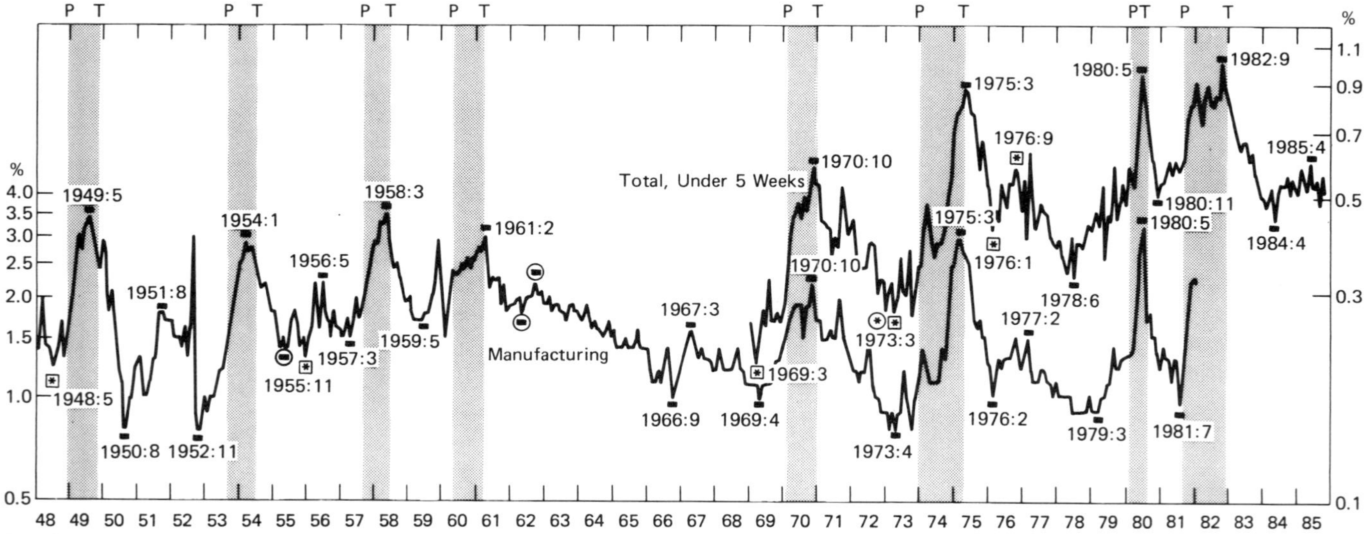

Layoff rates are adjusted for seasonal variations. Shaded areas are business cycle recessions, from peak (P) to trough (T). Asterisks mark cyclical peaks and troughs in the layoff rates as determined by computer program, modified by removing circled asterisks and inserting asterisks in squares.

Source: Center for International Business Cycle Research.

CHART 3–2
Layoff Rate and Initial Claims for Unemployment Insurance

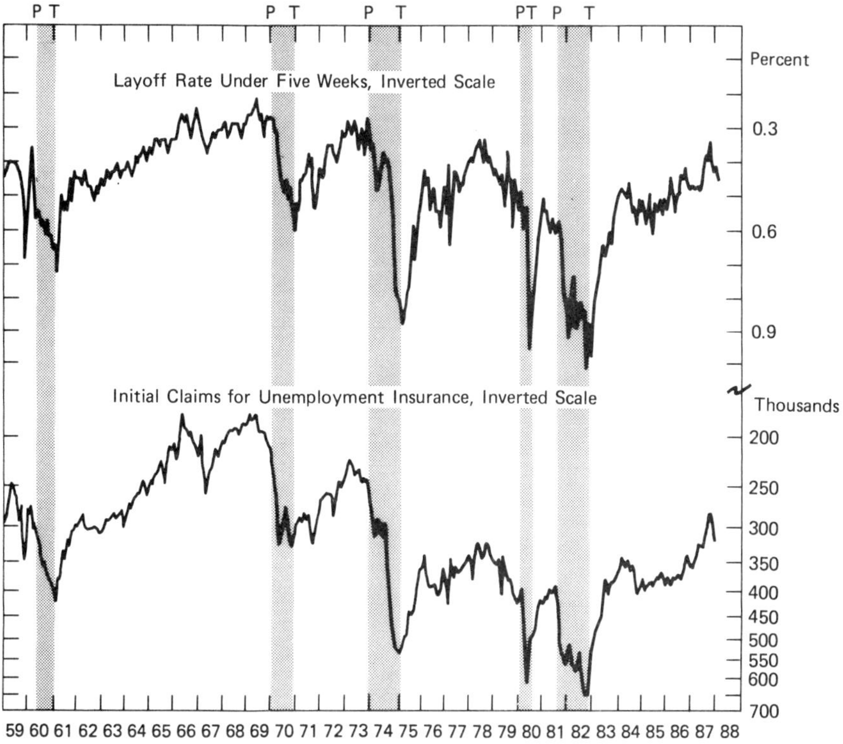

Shaded areas are business cycle recessions, from peak (P) to trough (T).

Its lead-lag record at business cycle peaks and troughs is shown in Table 3-1 (column 3), along with the records of the related series mentioned above. Relative to the manufacturing layoff rate during the overlapping period 1969–81, the new indicator shows longer leads at peaks and about the same at troughs. In view of their close relationship, we have linked the new rate after 1969 with the manufacturing rate before 1969. This forms a long series with one break in coverage (column 4). It leads at 14 of 16 business cycle turns from 1948 to 1982 and coincides twice, with an overall average lead of six months. The combined series is a more consistent leader than initial claims for unemployment insurance, which has coincident timing four times and lags twice during 1948–82 (column 5).

The new layoff rate also receives high grades in terms of prompt availability. Because it is a product of the household employment survey,

TABLE 3-1
Leads and Lags of Layoff Rates and
Initial Claims for Unemployment Insurance[1]

Business Cycle (1)		Layoff Rate, Manufacturing (2)		Layoff Rate, under 5 weeks (3)		Layoff Rate, Manufacturing, to 1968; Layoff Rate, under 5 weeks, since 1969 (4)		Initial Claims, Unemployment Insurance (5)	
P	T	P	T	P	T	P	T	P	T
11/48		−6				−6		−22	
	10/49		−5				−5		+1
7/53		−8				−8		−10	
	5/54		−4				−4		+4
8/57		−21				−21		−23	
	4/58		−1				−1		0
4/60		−11				−11		−12	
	2/61		0				0		0
12/69		−8		−9		−9		−11	
	11/70		−1		−1		−1		−1
11/73		−9		−2		−2		−9	
	3/75		−1		0		0		0
1/80		−11		−19		−19		−16	
	7/80		−2		−2		−2		−2
7/81		0		−8		−8		0	
	11/82		na		−2		−2		−2
Mean									
1969–81		−7	−1	−10	−1	−10	−1	−9	−1
			−5		−5		−5		−5
1948–82						−10	−2	−13	−3
							−6		−6
Standard deviation									
1948–82						6	2	7	2
							6		8
Percent Leads									
1969–81		75	100	100	75	100	75	75	75
			86		88		88		75
1948–82						100	75	88	38
							88		62

[1]Peaks in layoff rates and initial claims are matched with business cycle troughs and troughs in layoff rates and initial claims are matched with business cycle peaks. Abbreviations: P, peak; T, trough; na, not available.

Source: Center for International Business Cycle Research.

figures for the previous month are normally available on the first Friday of the following month. These figures are revised only once a year, when seasonal factors are changed. Initial claims are available weekly, with a two-week delay, which puts them on a par with the new layoff rate, although the monthly average is not available until the middle of the following month. However, erratic movements in the new layoff rate are relatively large, as the following measures show:

	I/C Ratio*	Months for Cyclical Dominance
New layoff rate, under 5 weeks, 1969–85	2.51	3
Manufacturing layoff rate, 1948–75	2.08	3
Initial claims, unemployment rate, 1948–75	1.95	2

*Ratio of irregular to cyclical amplitude, one-month span.

The layoff rate series tends to lead at business cycle peaks by much longer intervals than at troughs. In this respect it is similar to the unemployment rate, which leads at peaks but usually lags at troughs. The main reason for this asymmetry is that the business cycle dates are based upon data that reflect the rising long-run growth of the economy, whereas layoff and unemployment rates are relatively trendless. When the turns in the layoff rates are matched with those in the unemployment rate rather than the business cycle, the leads are more nearly symmetrical. The new layoff rate series leads the downturns in unemployment by an average of five months and the upturns by seven months, with an overall average lead of six months.

Compared with employment, the new layoff rate again leads at both peaks and troughs, but by much longer intervals at peaks. This is not surprising, because nonfarm employment is virtually coincident with the business cycle, reflecting the long-run rising growth trend of the economy.

One of the merits of the new layoff series compared with initial claims for unemployment insurance is that the latter, like the insured unemployment rate, is subject to changes in unemployment insurance regulations or practices. Moreover, changes can occur in the proportions of job losers who are eligible for unemployment insurance. In recent years, for example, initial claims and the number of insured unemployed have declined relative to the total number of unemployed. The layoff rate, on the other hand, has followed about the same trend as the total unemployment rate.

We recommend, therefore, that the Commerce Department include the new layoff rate among the indicators in the composite leading index in addition to initial claims. We also recommend that the formerly published subgroup index, marginal employment adjustments, be restored, including the layoff rate as well as initial claims, the average workweek, and overtime hours.

CHAPTER 4

CORPORATE BOND PRICES AS
A LEADING INDICATOR

Victor Zarnowitz

The Dow Jones index of corporate bond prices begins in 1915 and until 1975 covered 40 bonds, including 10 "higher-grade" railroad, 10 "second-grade" railroad, 10 public utility, and 10 industrial bonds. Since 1976, it includes 20 bonds, of which 10 are public utilities and 10 are industrials. Data are simple arithmetic averages of daily closing prices for each month, expressed in the form of an index ($1,000 = 100), not seasonally adjusted. They are published daily for the previous day, and monthly averages are published on the first working day of the following month. The sample of issues is changed as issues near maturity and for other reasons that might distort the price of particular issues.

The index led at each of the eight business cycle peaks since 1948 and at each of the eight troughs (Chart 4-1).[1] Its leads at business cycle peaks were very long and highly variable, ranging from 10 to 58 months

---

[1]This is so provided one accepts as a specific expansion the very short but also very sharp movement in bond prices between March and June 1980. (Note that the inverted yield on new high-grade corporate bond issues, BCD series 116, shows an exactly parallel pattern of change at the same time.) Excluding this somewhat marginal episode would yield the alternative inference that these series skipped the 1980 recession. However, it seems defensible to relax the timing rules and accept the leads in this case, given the unusually short duration of the recession in 1980 (six months from January to July) and the unusually large amplitude of the associated changes in bond prices and yields.

CHART 4–1 Corporate Bond Prices and Inverted Corporate Bond Yields

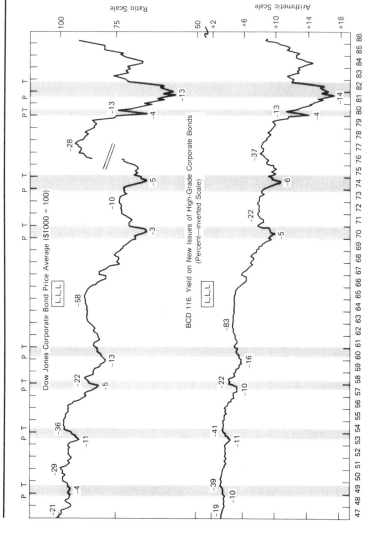

Dow Jones Corporate Bond Price Average ($1000 = 100)

BCD 116. Yield on New Issues of High-Grade Corporate Bonds
(Percent—Inverted Scale)

Ratio Scale

Arithmetic Scale

Shaded areas are business cycle recessions, from peak (P) to trough (T).

and averaging 27 months. Its leads at troughs were also long relative to the observed distributions of such leads and the durations of business cycle contractions: they ranged from 3 to 13 months and averaged 7 months. Only one pronounced extra movement occurred in bond prices since 1947 according to these data: a decline between May 1983 and July 1984.

Chart 4-1 illustrates the familiar inverse relationship between bond prices and bond yields by comparing the Dow Jones average with the yield on new issues of high-grade corporate bonds (BCD series 116). The two series tend to move together when the yields are plotted on an inverted scale. Both typically start rising in midcontraction or earlier, and both typically start falling in midexpansion or earlier. In some of the business expansions (1954–57, 1961–69, 1975–79) bond prices declined most of the time (i.e., the inverted behavior prevailed). The same applies to several business contractions during which bond prices moved mainly upward (1953–54, 1960–61, 1980, and 1981–82).

Inflation imparted a strong upward trend to interest rates in the post-World War II period, especially in the late 1960s and the 1970s when inflationary expectations spread widely at an accelerating rate. Accordingly, the series in Chart 4-1 show large downward trends, which contributes to the inverted elements in their cyclical behavior. On average, expansions in bond prices were shorter than contractions (24 versus 29 months), in strong contrast to the durations of business cycle expansions versus contractions in the same period (45 versus 11 months). For inverted yields, like bond prices, expansions are also shorter than contractions (20 versus 32 months). This suggests that the positive effect of business cycles on yields is stronger than the inverse effect of yields on business cycles.

The 27-month average lead of bond prices at peaks is 7 months less than the average lead of inverted yields, and the standard deviation is smaller also (Table 4-1). At troughs, the seven-month average lead of bond prices is three months less than the average lead of inverted yields, while the standard deviation is four months for both series. Inclusion of either of these series in the composite leading index would tend to increase its lead, a matter of some importance at troughs, where the leads are usually very short.

As estimated by the Bureau of Economic Analysis (BEA), the timing scores for the Dow Jones corporate bond price series are 83, 87, and 86 at peaks, troughs, and all turns, respectively. The scores for

TABLE 4-1

Corporate Bond Prices and Inverted Yields: Timing at Business Cycle Peaks and Troughs, 1948–82

| Line (1) | Business Cycle Peak (2) | Lead (−) or Lag (+) at Peak, in months | | Business Cycle Trough (5) | Lead (−) or Lag (+) at Troughs, in months | |
		Bond Prices (3)	Inverted Yields (4)		Bond Prices (6)	Inverted Yields (7)
1	11/48	−21	−19	10/49	−4	−10
2	7/53	−29	−39	5/54	−11	−11
3	8/57	−36	−41	4/60	−5	−10
4	4/60	−22	−22	2/61	−13	−16
5	12/69	−58	−83	11/70	−3	−5
6	11/73	−10	−22	3/75	−5	−6
7	1/80	−28	−37	7/80	−4	−4
8	7/81	−13	−13	11/82	−13	−14
9	Average	−27	−34		−7	−9
10	Standard deviation	15	22		4	4

Source: Dow Jones for bond prices, Citibank and U.S. Treasury for bond yields.

inverted yields are somewhat lower: 80, 84, and 83. Both series are classified as leaders at peaks, troughs, and overall (L,L,L). In general it appears that the bond price series would be the better of the two series to include in the leading index.

We have examined other available bond price series, including those compiled by Shearson-Lehman-Hutton, Merrill Lynch, and Salomon Brothers, but they do not have as long an historical record as the Dow Jones series. Chiefly for this reason we would recommend that the Dow Jones average be employed in the leading index. Because it has very long leads, it is also an obvious choice for a long-leading index.

CHAPTER 5

A NEW MONTHLY INDICATOR OF PROFIT MARGINS

Charlotte Boschan and Geoffrey H. Moore

Profit margins have long been classified as leading indicators. Four of them, all quarterly, are currently carried in BCD:

22. Ratio of corporate domestic profits after taxes to corporate domestic income (LLL).
81. Ratio of corporate domestic profits after taxes with IVA and CCA to corporate domestic income (ULL).
15. Profits after taxes per dollar of sales of manufacturing corporations (LLL).
26. Ratio of implicit price deflator to unit labor cost of the nonfarm business sector (LLL).

Because these series are available only quarterly, there is a considerable publication lag. As of mid-January, for example, the latest figures are for the third quarter. Also, series 22 and 15 reflect accounting profits rather than economic profits. Series 81, on the other hand, includes IVA (inventory valuation adjustments) and CCA (capital consumption adjustments) so that inventories are valued at replacement cost and capital depreciation is estimated on the basis of uniform service lives and replacement cost. Series 26 avoids these accounting problems and correlates well with Series 81 despite the fact that it takes account only of labor costs.

In order to surmount these difficulties, we have constructed a new price/unit labor cost ratio for manufacturing on a monthly basis. Heretofore the problem has been to obtain an appropriate price index. The manufactured goods component of the producer price index has not been suitable for this purpose, because it is weighted by sales and, hence, involves the double-counting of sales by some manufacturing industries to others. In January 1986, however, the BLS began publishing a new producer price index for manufacturing that eliminates intraindustry sales. That is, it uses net output (or value-added) weights for the year 1977. Conceptually, this makes it similar to the implicit price deflator used as the numerator of series 26, which covers all nonfarm business.

The BLS has published the net output price index only from December 1984 to date. To obtain a longer historical record we have estimated the index back to 1979, with results that appear reasonable. For this purpose the BLS supplied us with net output weights for all manufacturing industries in the Standard Industrial Classification (SIC) on a four-digit level, as well as with back data for producer price indexes for these industries starting as early as possible and ending in February 1986. Some series start as early as 1920, but most of them became available during the 70s and 80s. By January 1979, 168 price series were available with a combined contribution to the total manufacturing index of about 56 percent. Petroleum prices are included in this list, but because of their extraordinary movements in 1979 and large weight in the sample of price series available, we concluded after some experimentation that the index would be more representative of total manufacturing if they were omitted. Between 1979 and 1984, therefore, our price index covers 167 series with a weight of 45 percent in the total index. In order to maintain consistency over this six-year span, we kept the list of price series constant and did not add industries as data became available. The estimated index was computed by weighting the industry price indexes by their respective net output weights.

A comparison of our index, January 1979 to February 1986, with the BLS's price index for manufacturing net output, December 1984 through 1986, is shown in Chart 5-1. In view of their similarity, we judged it appropriate to splice the two series in January 1985.

For the period prior to 1979 we have constructed a quarterly price deflator for net output in manufacturing by interpolating the existing annual deflator for gross product originating in manufacturing, using the

CHART 5–1
New Indexes of Net Output Prices, Manufacturing

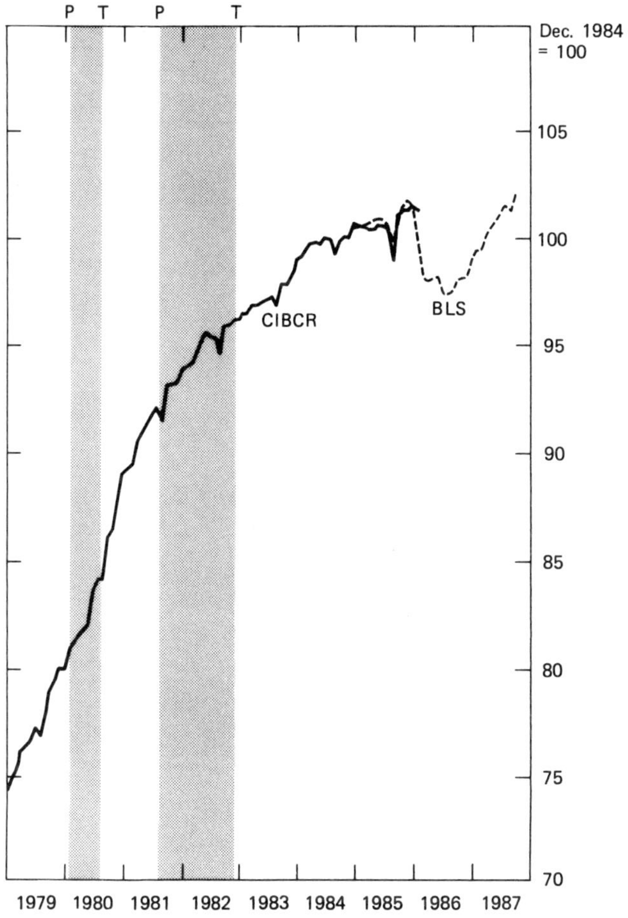

Shaded areas are business cycle recessions, from peak (P) to trough (T). CIBCR, Center for International Business Cycle Research; BLS, Bureau of Labor Statistics.

BLS quarterly deflator for nonfarm business output as the interpolator. Because the new quarterly series and the monthly net output price indexes correspond closely, we put the three components into a single index that is quarterly from 1948 to 1978 and monthly from 1979 to date (Chart 5-2).

CHART 5–2
New Indexes of Prices and Unit Labor Cost, Manufacturing

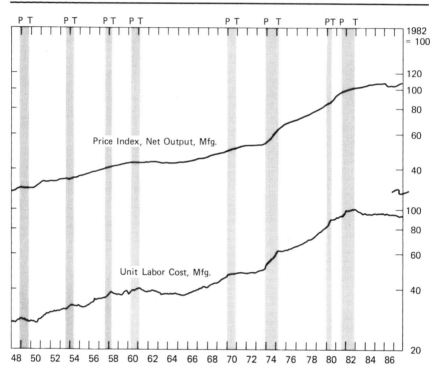

Shaded areas are business cycle recessions, from peak (P) to trough (T).

Although originally we assumed that a price/unit labor cost ratio for manufacturing could be derived by dividing the above price index by the existing monthly unit labor cost series for manufacturing (BCD series 62), we have found that the result is not satisfactory. The cost series has a downward bias because of an upward bias in the output figures used in the denominator. That is, the monthly FRB index of manufacturing production has an upward trend relative to the annual Commerce Department figures on real gross product originating in manufacturing. To illustrate, the annual growth rates in the two series since 1947 are as follows:

Percent Change, at Annual Rate

	Real Gross Domestic Product, Manufacturing	Index of Production, Manufacturing
1947–57	3.9	4.5
1957–67	4.1	5.0
1967–77	2.6	3.2
1977–85	2.4	3.0

Hence we adjusted the monthly output figures to reflect the annual movements in real gross product, following the same procedure used by BLS to obtain its quarterly series on manufacturing output. The resulting monthly series on unit labor cost has the same movements as the quarterly BLS index of unit labor cost in manufacturing, and we use it to obtain the price/labor cost ratio quarterly 1948–78 and monthly from 1979. The new monthly series on unit labor cost should also be used to replace the unit labor cost series in the lagging index (see Chapter 14).

Despite the fact that the new price/labor cost ratio is limited to manufacturing, Chart 5-3 shows that it conforms well with the quarterly series on corporate profit margins (BCD series 81) and the price/labor cost ratio for nonfarm business (BCD series 26). This point is also supported by Chart 5-4, which compares the new price/unit labor cost series for manufacturing with two quarterly series for all nonfinancial corporations. Here we see that for the same corporate universe, the price/unit labor cost ratio is a good proxy for profits per dollar of output. Also, the new series for manufacturing is closely correlated with both of the quarterly corporate series. These quarterly series are derived from data published by the BLS in its productivity estimates.[1] Because they are more comparable with one another than series 81 and 26, the BEA might consider using them in BCD.

---

[1]Profits per dollar of output is derived by dividing the reported profits per unit of output by the implicit price deflator in order to express output in current dollars.

CHART 5–3
Three Indicators of Profit Margins

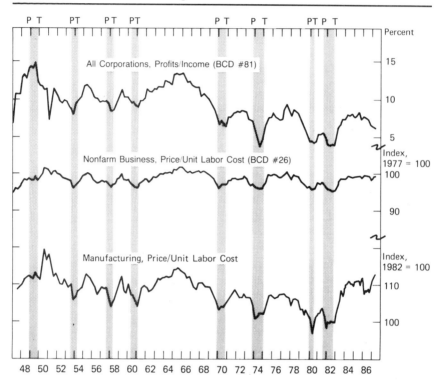

Shaded areas are business cycle recessions, from peak (P) to trough (T). BCD, *Business Conditions Digest.*

The new price/unit labor cost ratio for manufacturing has long and reasonably consistent leads at both business cycle peaks and troughs (Table 5-1). A preliminary estimate of the ratio for the preceding month, based on wages of production workers instead of wages and salaries of all employees, is usually available by the 19th of the following month. We, therefore, recommend the price/unit labor cost ratio as a new component of the BCD leading index. It qualifies also for the standards we have set for the long-leading index (see Chapter 9).

CHART 5–4
Price/Cost Ratios and Profit Margins

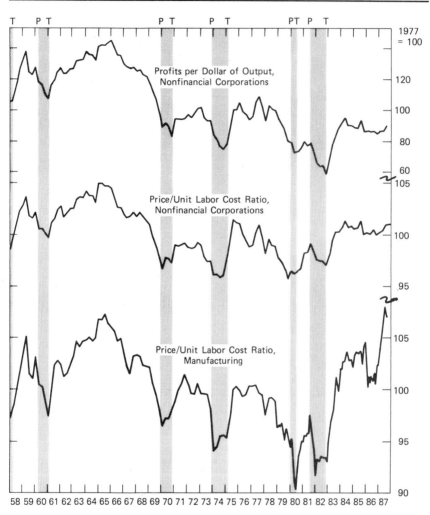

Shaded areas are business cycle recessions, from peak (P) to trough (T).

TABLE 5-1
Lead/Lag Record of Price/Unit Labor Cost, Manufacturing

Business Cycle		Price/Cost Ratio, Manufacturing		Lead(−) or Lag (+) of Price/Cost Ratio	
Peak	Trough	Peak	Trough	Peak	Trough
11/48		—		—	
	10/49		—		—
7/53		8/50		−35	
	5/54		11/53		−6
8/57		5/55		−27	
	4/58		2/58		−2
4/60		5/59		−11	
	2/61		2/61		0
12/69		8/65		−52	
	11/70		2/70		−9
11/73		11/71		−24	
	3/75		2/74		−13
1/80		5/77		−32	
	7/80		6/80		−1
7/81		7/81		0	
	11/82		1/82		−10
Mean				−26	−6
				−16	
Standard deviation				16	5
				15	
Percentage leads				86	86
				86	

CHAPTER 6

IMPROVED MEASURES OF INVENTORIES AND DELIVERIES

Philip A. Klein and Geoffrey H. Moore

INVENTORY INVESTMENT

One of the components of the BCD leading index has been the change in manufacturing and trade inventories on hand and on order in 1982 dollars (series 36). The figures are smoothed by a weighted four-month moving average, because the month-to-month changes are very erratic. The moving averages are placed in the terminal month of the span, so the resulting series is just as up-to-date as the monthly change from which it is derived, although the smoothing process tends to make it lag a bit. Nevertheless, one of the major problems with the series is the publication delay. The current month's figure is not available at the time the BCD index is compiled, and this leads to a revision of the index the following month when the missing figure is available. If this could be avoided, the revisions of the index would be substantially smaller.

The survey of inventories conducted by the NAPM provides a way out of this difficulty. The survey is published early in the month following the month to which the figures pertain, so the survey is available about three weeks before the leading index is compiled. The survey is also available about five weeks before the inventory change figures for the same month. The question, then, is: Does the NAPM series perform satisfactorily as a leading indicator?

TABLE 6-1
Cyclical Timing of Inventory Change and the NAPM Survey of Inventories

Business Cycle (1)		Inventory Change, Smoothed[1] (2)		NAPM Survey Inventories (3)		Leads (−) and Lags (+), in Months					
						Inventory Change vs. Business Cycle (4)		NAPM Survey vs. Business Cycle (5)		NAPM Survey vs. Inventory Change (6)	
P	T	P	T	P	T	P	T	P	T	P	T
11/48	10/49	7/48	6/49	6/48	7/49	−4	−4	−5	−3	−1	+1
—		4/51	—	7/50	5/52	—		—		−9	—
7/53	5/54	—	11/53	3/53	2/54	−27*	−6	−4	−3	—	+3
8/57	4/58	9/56	3/58	6/55	5/58	−11	−1	−26	+1	−1.	+2
4/60	2/61	4/59	2/61	6/59	2/61	−12	0	−10	0	+2	0
—		—		1/62	1/64	—		—		—	—
—		4/66	—	2/65	7/67	—		—		−14	—
12/69	11/70	—	3/70	11/69	5/70	−44**	−8	−1	−6	—	+2
11/73	3/75	4/73	4/75	10/73	7/75	−7	+1	−1	+4	+6	+3

TABLE 6-1—Continued

Leads (−) and Lags (+), in Months (columns 4–6)

Business Cycle (1)		Inventory Change, Smoothed¹ (2)		NAPM Survey Inventories (3)		Inventory Change vs. Business Cycle (4)		NAPM Survey vs. Business Cycle (5)		NAPM Survey vs. Inventory Change (6)	
P	T	P	T	P	T	P	T	P	T	P	T
1/80	7/80	1/79	8/80	7/78	7/80	−12	+1	−18	0	−6	−1
7/81	11/82	7/81	1/83	6/81	5/82	0	+2	−1	−6	−1	−8
		4/84		12/83							
Mean at P&T						−15	−8	−8	−5	−5	−2
Median at P&T						−12	−5	−4	−3	−4	−1
Percentage leads at P&T						88	69	100	75	78	53

*4/51 peak compared with 7/53 peak.
**4/66 peak compared with 12/69 peak.
¹Monthly change in manufacturing and trade inventories on hand and on order in 1982 dollars, smoothed by weighted four-month moving average (*Business Conditions Digest* series 36).
Abbreviations: NAPM, National Association of Purchasing Management; P, peak; T, trough.

Chart 6-1 compares the NAPM series with the smoothed inventory change. Both series are quite volatile and show a number of extra cycles. Table 6-1 compares the timing of the two series with business cycles and with each other. The inventory change series has somewhat longer leads than the survey series at peaks, whereas the two are virtually the same vis-a-vis the business cycle at troughs. However, when the two series are compared directly, including the extra cycles that do not match the business cycle, the survey leads the actual change more often than not at peaks, whereas they are roughly coincident at troughs. In terms of cyclical behavior, therefore, the two series are very similar. This is supported by correlogram analysis, which yields a maximum r^2 of .48 when the two series are coincident.

CHART 6–1
NAPM Survey of Inventories Versus Change in Manufacturing and Trade Inventories

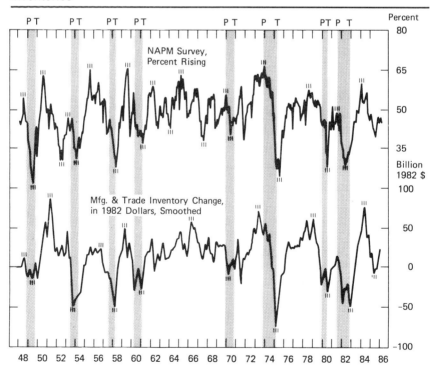

Shaded areas are business cycle recessions, from peak (P) to trough (T). NAPM, National Association of Purchasing Management.

In view of these results we recommend that the NAPM inventory survey series be substituted for the inventory change series currently used in the Commerce Department's leading index. Of course, the inventory change series should continue to be published in BCD, because it is valuable for analytical purposes where timeliness is not a factor.

VENDOR PERFORMANCE

Another useful leading indicator is vendor performance, which is the percentage of companies reporting slower deliveries. When this in-

CHART 6–2
Vendor Performance Versus the Ratio of Sales to Inventories

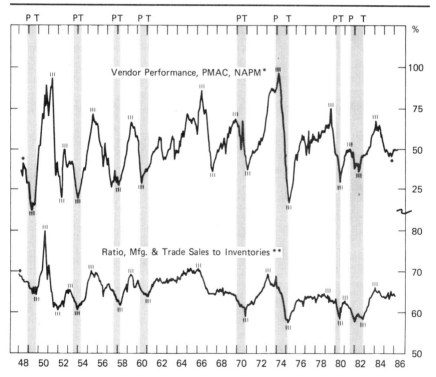

Shaded areas are business cycle recessions, from peak (P) to trough (T). PMAC, Purchasing Management Association of Chicago; NAPM, National Association of Purchasing Management.
*Percent reporting slower deliveries.
**Monthly sales as a percent of inventories.

TABLE 6-2
Cyclical Timing of Sales/Inventory Ratio and Vendor Performance Survey

Business Cycle (1)		Sales/Inventory Ratio[1] (2)		Vendor Performance[2] (3)		Leads (−) and Lags (+), in months					
						Sales/Inventory Ratio vs. Business Cycle (4)		Vendor Performance vs. Business Cycle (5)		Vendor Performance vs. Sales/Inventory Ratio (6)	
P	T	P	T	P	T	P	T	P	T	P	T
11/48	10/49	1/48	10/49	4/48	3/49	−10	0	−7	−7	+3	−7
—	—	7/50	12/51	2/51	3/52	—	—	—	—	+7	+3
7/53	5/54	3/53	12/53	7/52	11/53	−4	−5	−12	−6	−8	−1
8/57	4/58	4/55	12/53	4/55	12/57	−28	0	−28	−4	0	−4
4/60	2/61	5/59	1/61	2/59	3/60	−11	−1	−14	−11	−3	−10
—	—	1/66	—	3/66	5/67	—	—	—	—	+2	—
12/69	11/70	—	11/70	8/69	12/70	−47*	0	−4	+1	—	+1
11/73	3/75	2/73	3/75	11/73	2/75	−9	0	0	−1	+9	−1

TABLE 6-2—Continued

Business Cycle (1)		Sales/ Inventory Ratio[1] (2)		Vendor Performance[2] (3)		Sales/Inventory Ratio vs. Business Cycle (4)		Vendor Performance vs. Business Cycle (5)		Vendor Performance vs. Sales/Inventory Ratio (6)	
P	*T*	*P*	*T*	*P*	*T*	*P*	*T*	*P*	*T*	*P*	*T*
1/80		3/79		4/79		−10		−9		+1	
	7/80		6/80		5/80		−1		−2		−1
7/81		1/81		4/81		−6		−3		+3	
	11/82		10/82		3/82		−1		−8		−7
			1/84	11/83						−2	
Mean at P&T						−16	−8	−10	−7	+1	−1
Median at P&T						−10	−4	−8	−6	+2	−1
Percentage leads at P&T						100	75	88	88	30	53

*1/66 peak compared to 12/69 peak.

[1] Ratio of manufacturing and trade sales to inventories in 1982 dollars (reciprocal of *Business Conditions Digest* series 77).

[2] Percentage reporting slower deliveries, Purchasing Management Association of Chicago through 1975, National Association of Purchasing Management from 1976. Data are seasonally adjusted.

Abbreviations: P, peak; T, trough.

creases, it is a sign of expanding economic activity, with order backlogs piling up or sales outrunning inventories. The series presently used in the BCD leading index is compiled by the Purchasing Management Association of Chicago (PMAC) in a survey covering companies in the greater Chicago area. Beginning in 1976 a similar series with national coverage is available from the NAPM, and we have linked the two series at that date (Chart 6-2).

It is of interest to compare vendor performance with the ratio of sales to inventories, the reciprocal of the inventory/sales ratio that is presently used as a lagging indicator (BCD series 77). When vendors' sales/inventory ratios are high, deliveries may slow down since vendors will be depending more on production to fill orders. The series are compared in Chart 6-2 and their leads and lags are recorded in Table 6-2. The chart suggests that the two series are reasonably closely related. Vendor performance has longer leads on average at business cycle troughs, whereas the sales/inventory ratio has longer leads at peaks. This is confirmed in column 6 of the table, which shows that vendor performance leads the ratio at troughs but lags at peaks. A correlogram analysis, which of course does not distinguish troughs from peaks, yields a maximum correlation when the series are viewed as coincident, but the r^2 is only .27.

In short, both series contribute information about the business cycle, and both are leading indicators, although vendor performance is more consistent in this respect. A further point to be noted is that the vendor performance survey is available on a timely basis, whereas the sales/inventory ratio is subject to the same publication lag as noted above for inventory change. We recommend that the linked PMAC-NAPM vendor performance series be used in the BCD leading index.

CHAPTER 7

A NEW INDUSTRIAL MATERIALS PRICE INDEX

Geoffrey H. Moore

An index of industrial materials prices designed and constructed by CIBCR has been published daily by the *Journal of Commerce* since September 1986. It includes the prices of 18 important materials used in manufacturing, energy production, and building construction. Compared with other available indexes of this type, it covers a broader, more modern range of products, such as crude petroleum, aluminum, polyester and plywood (see Table 7-1). Subgroup indexes covering textiles, metals, petroleum products, and miscellaneous commodities are also compiled. The commodities were selected on the basis of a review of their economic significance and their performance as leading indicators of inflation (CPI). Much of this underlying research was conducted by Geoffrey Joyce at CIBCR. The index has been compiled monthly back to January 1948, using standardization and weighting procedures similar to those used by the Commerce Department in its composite indexes. This produces a less erratic index.

As compared with the sensitive price index (BCD series 99) currently used in the Commerce Department's leading index, the new index has the advantage of avoiding internal duplication, since BCD series 99 is an average of two indexes with overlapping coverage (see Table 7-1). Another difference is that the new index includes petroleum prices, which since the 1970s have become of enormous significance to both business activity and inflation. Because the price series included in the new index

TABLE 7-1
Components of Three Indexes of Industrial Materials Prices[1]

18 Commodities Index, JOC	13 Commodities Index, BLS/CRB (BCD Series 23)	28 Commodities Index, BEA (BCD Series 98)
	Textiles	
Cotton	Cotton	Cotton
Burlap	Burlap	Hard fibers
Printcloth	Printcloth	
Polyester		
	Wool tops	Wool (3 series)
	Metals	
Steel scrap	Steel scrap	Iron and steel scrap (7 series)
Copper scrap	Copper scrap	Copper scrap
Lead	Lead scrap	Other nonferrous scrap
Zinc	Zinc	
Tin	Tin	
Aluminum		Aluminum scrap
	Petroleum Products	
Crude oil		
Benzene		
	Miscellaneous	
Hides	Hides	Hides
Rubber	Rubber	Rubber
Tallow	Tallow	
Plywood	Rosin	Lumber (4 series)
Red oak		
Old corrugated boxes		Wastepaper (6 series)
		Sand, gravel, and crushed stone

[1]BCD series 99, change in sensitive materials prices, is an average of BCD series 23 and BCD series 98.
Abbreviations: JOC, *Journal of Commerce*; BLS, Bureau of Labor Statistics; CRB, Commodities Research Bureau; BCD, *Business Conditions Digest*; BEA, Bureau of Economic Analysis.

were selected on the basis of their significance and performance as leading indicators of inflation, the growth rate in the index has a consistent record of leading the inflation rate (CPI). In addition, however, it qualifies as a leading indicator of business cycles. Since 1949, it has led business cycle peaks by an average of 11 months and troughs by 3 months. It led at 10 of the 16 turns, lagged twice, and skipped 4 turns (Table 7-2). On five occasions it declined significantly when there was no recession.

CHART 7–1
Growth Rates in Industrial Materials Price Indexes

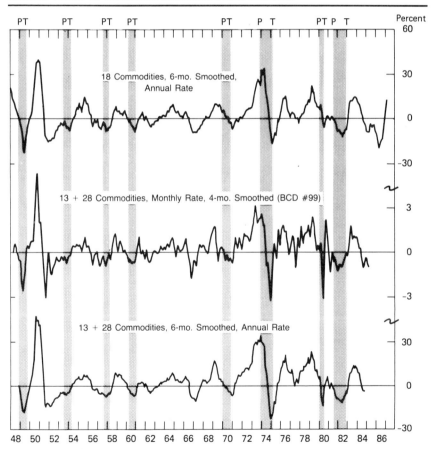

Shaded areas are business cycle recessions, from peak (P) to trough (T). BCD, *Business Conditions Digest.*

TABLE 7-2
Lead/Lag Record of Growth Rates of Two Industrial Materials Price Indexes

Business Cycle		18 Commodities Index, Six-Month Smoothed Rate				Lead (−) or Lag (+) in months		28 + 13 Commodities Index			
		Date of		Growth Rate (%)				Four-Month Smoothed Rate		Six-Month Smoothed Rate	
P	T	P	T	P	T	P	T	P	T	P	T
11/48		1/48*		19.5		−10		−4		na	
	10/49		6/49		−23.0		−4		−5		−4
7/53		ntc		ntc		ntc		ntc		ntc	
	5/54		ntc		ntc		ntc		ntc		ntc
8/57		9/55		14.9		−23		−23		−23	
	4/58		11/57		−8.8		−5		−5		−5
4/60		11/58		8.8		−17		−18		−17	
	2/61		12/60		−9.0		−2		−6		−3
12/69		3/69		10.2		−9		−10		−9	
	11/70		12/70		−7.1		+1		+2		+1
11/73		3/74		34.1		+4		−7		+1	
	3/75		1/75		−16.7		−2		−2		−2
1/80		3/79		22.4		−10		−9		−10	
	7/80		ntc		ntc		ntc		−1		−1
7/81		ntc		ntc		ntc		−9		−8	
	11/82		6/82		−12.1		−5		−11		−5

48

TABLE 7-2—Continued

	Business Cycle		18 Commodities Index, Six-Month Smoothed Rate						28 + 13 Commodities Index			
			Date of		Growth Rate (%)		Lead (−) or Lag (+) in months		Four-Month Smoothed Rate		Six-Month Smoothed Rate	
	P	T	P	T	P	T	P	T	P	T	P	T
Mean												
P							−11		−11		−11	
T								−3		−4		−3
All turns							−7		−8		−7	
Standard deviation												
P							8.3		6.2		7.5	
T								2.8		3.9		2.1
All turns							7.2		6.3		6.7	
Percentage leads												
P							83		100		86	
T								83		86		86
All turns							83		93		85	
Extra cycles			11/50	11/51	39.7	−15.7			9/50	9/51	9/50	2/52
			9/61	7/62	4.6	−6.0			5/61	6/61	9/61	7/62
			11/64	3/67	9.3	−9.7			3/66	10/66	10/64	4/67
			7/76	11/77	15.4	−3.3			4/76	7/77	7/76	6/77
			9/83	3/86	15.0	−19.7			4/83	8/84	8/83	8/84

*Growth rate data begin January 1948; hence peak may have been earlier.
Abbreviations: P, peak; T, trough; na, not available; ntc, no timing comparison.

The leads of the six-month smoothed growth rate of the 18 Commodities Index are often a month or so shorter than those of BCD series 99 because of the difference in smoothing method. The monthly changes in BCD series 99 are smoothed by a four-month moving average, with weights 1, 2, 2, and 1, and placed in the terminal month. When the six-month smoothed growth rate is used for BCD series 99, the turns are a bit later and nearly identical with those in the new index (Table 7-2 and Chart 7-1).

Although there is little to choose between the new index and BCD series 99 on grounds of performance when both are smoothed the same way, we believe the new index is superior in content and method of construction and easier for users to follow since it is published daily. We, therefore, recommend that it replace BCD series 99 in the leading index.

CHAPTER 8

NEW MEASURES OF THE GROWTH OF DEBT

Victor Zarnowitz and Geoffrey H. Moore

In the Commerce Department's leading index, the growth of debt is represented by the month-to-month percentage change in business and consumer credit outstanding (BCD series 111). Its principal deficiencies as a leading indicator are that it is quite erratic, and since 1958, it has not shown a clear tendency to lead at troughs. The record at troughs from 1958 to 1982 shows two leads of one and two months, two coincidences, and two lags of one and two months (see Table 8-1). Our efforts to improve the series by weighting its components, employing a six-month smoothed growth rate, and deflating the debt to allow for inflation produce a smoother series but not a leader at troughs. We recommend that the six-month smoothed growth rates of the weighted and deflated series be used in BCD, though not in the leading index (see Chart 8-1).

By broadening the scope of the debt series, it is possible to obtain a measure that leads at both peaks and troughs. The broadest such measure is domestic nonfinancial debt, compiled monthly by the FRB. In deflated form, the growth rate in this series leads at every peak and trough since 1958 except for 1981–82. It did not conform sufficiently well to this recession for a peak and trough to be identified (see Chart 8-2). It is an unfortunate lapse, because this was a severe recession. The inflation rate declined so sharply that even though the growth in nominal debt de-

TABLE 8-1
Growth Rates in Business and Consumer Debt, with Smoothed and Deflated Variants, Timing at Business Cycle Turns, 1948–82

Business Cycle		Lead (−) or Lag (+), in Months					
		Change in Business and Consumer Debt (BCD Series 111)[1]		Six-Month Smoothed Rate of Business and Consumer Debt[2]		Six-Month Smoothed Rate of Business and Consumer Debt, Deflated[2]	
P	T	P	T	P	T	P	T
11/48		−12		na		na	
	10/49		−3		−2		−1
7/53		−9		−3		−3	
	5/54		−5		+3		+3
8/57		−26		−23		−24	
	4/58		−2		+1		0
4/60		−10		−8		−8	
	2/61		+2		+5		+5
12/69		−11		−8		−7	
	11/70		−1		0		0
11/73		−9		−8		−9	
	3/75		0		+3		+4
1/80		−12		−19		−25	
	7/80		0		+1		−1
7/81		−2		+1		+9	
	11/82		+1		+6		+1
Median		−10	0	−8	+2	−8	0
Mean		−11	−1	−10	+2	−10	+1
Standard deviation		6.7	2.3	8.5	2.6	11.9	2.3
Percentage leads		100	50	86	12	86	25
Extra turns		3	2	3	2	3	2

[1]Month-to-month change at annual rate, unweighted. The timing measures for the weighted series, where different, are as follows: peak, 1/80, −22; trough, 7/80, −2; mean (SD), −13(7.7) at peaks, −1(2.2) at troughs; median at troughs, −2; percentage leads at troughs, 62.

[2]Based on the weighted series computed by Center for International Business Cycle Research. Deflated series is obtained by dividing debt by the consumer price index. Abbreviations: na = not available; P = peak, T = trough.

clined during the recession, the growth in real value of the debt continued to accelerate. The growth of federal debt was a big factor in producing this result. In deflated form, federal debt accelerated rapidly throughout the 1981–82 recession.

Although we believe that the growth rate in deflated domestic

CHART 8–1

Three Measures of the Growth of Business and Consumer Debt

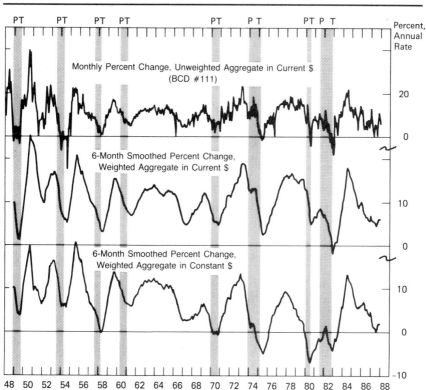

Shaded areas are business cycle recessions, from peak (P) to trough (T). BCD, *Business Conditions Digest.*

nonfinancial debt has an acceptable record as a leading indicator, the debt figures are not presently published by the Federal Reserve promptly enough to be available at the time the Commerce Department's leading index is compiled. We understand, however, that the staffs of the two agencies are undertaking to develop an estimating procedure so that a preliminary figure would be available on a timely basis. If that does not prove feasible, an alternative would be to use the aggregate of business, consumer, and federal debt that has been compiled monthly by the CIBCR.

CHART 8–2
Growth Rates in Public and Private Debt

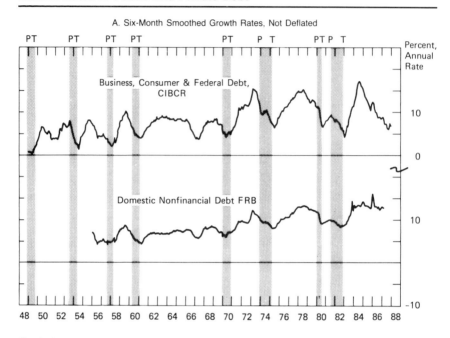

A. Six-Month Smoothed Growth Rates, Not Deflated

Shaded areas are business cycle recessions, from peak (P) to trough (T). CIBCR, Center for International Business Cycle Research; FRB, Federal Reserve Board.

The chief difference between the CIBCR series and the FRB series is that the former does not include corporate bonds or state and local bonds. Figures for these types of debt are subject to longer delays. The business and consumer debt component is similar to BCD series 111 except that the CIBCR series is a weighted aggregate. The weighting procedure is important, because federal debt is included in its entirety and would otherwise be overweighted. Chart 8-2 and Table 8-2 compare the CIBCR and FRB aggregates. The timing records of the growth rates are very similar, so much so that in columns 9 and 10 of the table we have consolidated the two deflated series, using the CIBCR series prior to 1956 when the FRB series is not available.

Some concern may be felt that the inclusion of federal debt, or total federal, state, and local debt in a business indicator is inappropriate and that total private debt would be superior for this purpose. It is true that the

CHART 8–2—*Continued*

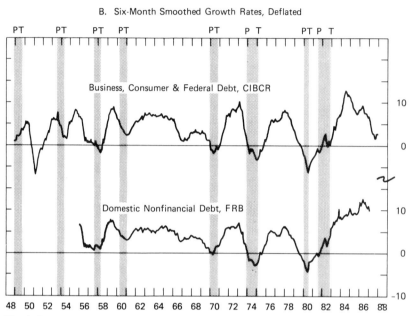

B. Six-Month Smoothed Growth Rates, Deflated

Business, Consumer & Federal Debt, CIBCR

Domestic Nonfinancial Debt, FRB

48 50 52 54 56 58 60 62 64 66 68 70 72 74 76 78 80 82 84 86 88

Shaded areas are business cycle recessions, from peak (P) to trough (T). CIBCR, Center for International Business Cycle Research; FRB, Federal Reserve Board.

growth rate of federal debt does not display very consistent properties as a cyclical indicator (Chart 8-3). Its movements are largely inverse to the business cycle, at least partly because of the decline in revenue and increases in unemployment compensation payments during recessions. The inverse movements may also reflect policy decisions to combat recession or inflation. Under certain conditions, the expansion of federal debt may raise interest rates and have "crowding out" effects on private borrowing and investment.

In any event, it appears to us that the strongest argument for using an aggregate that includes both public and private debt is that the creation of credit is similar in many ways to the creation of money, and it is the total volume of credit, like money, that is most relevant to the fluctuations in the overall economy. This relationship underlies the decision by the FRB in February 1982 to monitor a credit aggregate, namely, domestic nonfinancial debt, along with measures of the stock of money, as a guide to

TABLE 8-2
Six-Month Smoothed Growth Rates in Broad Aggregates of Debt in Current and Constant Dollars, Timing at Business Cycle Turns, 1948–82[1]

Business Cycle		Lead (−) or Lag (+), in Months							
		Business, Consumer, and Federal Debt (CIBCR)*		Business, Consumer, and Federal Debt, Deflated (CIBCR)		Total Domestic Nonfinancial Debt (FRB)		Total Domestic Nonfinancial Debt, Deflated (FRB, CIBCR)	
(1) P	(2) T	(3) P	(4) T	(5) P	(6) T	(7) P	(8) T	(9) P	(10) T
11/48	10/49	na	−3	na	−3	na	na	na	−3
7/53	5/54	0	+2	0	+2	na	na	0	+2
8/57	4/58	−23	−2	−25	−1	na	−6	−25	−1
4/60	2/61	−8	+2	−9	−1	−8	+2	−12	−1
12/69	11/70	−8	−7	−19	−7	−14	−7	−23	−7
11/73	3/75	−8	+3	−9	−3	−9	+3	−9	−3
1/80	7/80	−19	0	−25	−1	−17	0	−23	−1
7/81	11/82	−1	+1	nm	nm	−1	−4	nm	nm

56

TABLE 8-2—Continued

Business Cycle		Lead (−) or Lag (+), in Months							
		Business, Consumer, and Federal Debt (CIBCR)*		Business, Consumer, and Federal Debt, Deflated (CIBCR)		Total Domestic Nonfinancial Debt (FRB)		Total Domestic Nonfinancial Debt, Deflated (FRB, CIBCR)	
(1) P	*(2)* T	*(3)* P	*(4)* T	*(5)* P	*(6)* T	*(7)* P	*(8)* T	*(9)* P	*(10)* T
Median		−8	0	−9	−1	−9	−2	−18	−1
Mean		−10	0	−14	−2	−10	−2	−15	−2
Standard deviation		8.6	3.3	9.2	2.6	6.1	4.2	9.1	2.6
Percentage leads		86	38	83	86	100	50	83	86
Number skipped turns		0	0	1	1	0	0	1	1
Number extra turns		3	2	3	2	1	1	3	2

[1]The deflated series are obtained by dividing the outstanding debt, seasonally adjusted, by the seasonally adjusted consumer price index. The entries in columns 9 and 10 for 1949–57 are obtained from those in columns 5 and 6 (see text).
Abbreviations: CIBCR, Center for International Business Cycle Research; FRB, Federal Reserve Board; na, not available; nm, no matching turn; P, Peak; T, Trough.

CHART 8–3
Growth Rates in Federal Debt

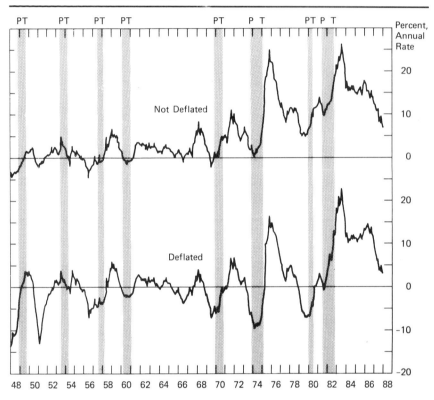

Shaded areas are business cycle recessions, from peak (P) to trough (T).

monetary policy. The observed tendency of the flow of credit, as reflected in the growth of debt, to lead the turns in the business cycle (as
well as the inflation cycle) supports the view that movements in total debt
have an important impact. We recommend, therefore, that the growth rate
of total public and private debt, measured as discussed above, be considered for inclusion in the leading index. Use of the deflated series would
be consistent with the decision taken some years ago to target the real
economy in the indicator system.

CHAPTER 9

LONG–LEADING AND SHORT–LEADING INDEXES

John P. Cullity and Geoffrey H. Moore

This chapter sketches the development of long-leading and short-leading composite indexes for the United States. It begins with a description of the components included in the long-leading index. The four components are (1) the Dow Jones 20-bond price index; (2) a new monthly series on the ratio of price to unit labor cost in manufacturing; (3) the money supply (M2) in constant (1982) dollars; and (4) building permits for new housing.

An excellent economic rationale exists for each of these components and details on this are provided in a longer paper.[1] The building permits and the money supply series are components of the Commerce Department's leading composite index. The bond price index and the new price/cost ratio series are discussed in Chapters 4 and 5. Each long-leading indicator was required to have an average lead of at least 12 months at peaks and 6 months at troughs for the business cycles from 1948 to 1982. Not many leading indicators can pass this test. The average leads of the long-leading series as well as those with shorter leads are shown in Table 9-1.

---

[1]See J. P. Cullity and G. H. Moore, "Developing a Long-Leading Composite Index for the United States," paper presented at the 18th CIRET (Centre for International Research on Economic Tendency Surveys) Conference, Zurich, Switzerland, September 10, 1987. The paper appears in *Contributions of Business Cycle Surveys to Empirical Economics,* Avebury, Gower Publishing Co., Brookfield, Vt., 1988.

TABLE 9-1
Average Leads at Business Cycle Turning Points:
Long Leaders and Short Leaders

BCD Series No.	Series	Average Lead (−), in months, at		
		P	T	P&T
	A. Long Leaders			
	Bond prices, Dow Jones	−27	−7	−17
	Ratio, price/unit labor cost, manufacturing	−26	−6	−16
106	Money supply (M2), constant dollars	−17	−6	−11
29	Building permits, housing	−15	−6	−10
	B. Short Leaders			
	Change in deflated nonfinancial debt	−17	−2	−9
19	Stock price index, S&P 500	−9	−5	−7
1	Average workweek, manufacturing	−10	−2	−6
	Layoff rate under five weeks	−10	−2	−6
5	Initial claims, unemployment insurance	−13	0	−6
8	New orders, consumer goods and materials	−8	−4	−6
	NAPM vendor performance	−8	−5	−6
	NAPM inventory change	−8	−2	−6
	Change in material prices, *Journal of Commerce*	−8	−2	−6
	Change in business population, CIBCR	−9	−2	−5
20	Contracts and orders, plant and equipment	−6	−1	−3
	C. Leading Indexes			
	Long-leading index, CIBCR	−14	−8	−11
	Short-leading index, CIBCR	−8	−2	−5
	Leading index, BCD	−10	−3	−6

Abbreviations: BCD, *Business Conditions Digest;* P, peaks; T, troughs; NAPM, National Association of Purchasing Management; CIBCR, Center for International Business Cycle Research.

Source: *Business Conditions Digest*, U.S. Department of Commerce, and Center for International Business Cycle Research, Columbia Business School. The long-leading index, CIBCR, includes the four series in section A, above. The short-leading index, CIBCR, includes the 11 series in section B.

The average lead of the long-leading composite index is 14 months at peaks and 8 months at troughs. It leads the Commerce Department's leading composite by four months at peaks and five months at troughs. It seems plain that the new long-leading composite could help solve one of the problems associated with the Commerce index, that is, its very short lead at cyclical troughs, often only one or two months (see Table 9-2).

Chart 9-1 shows the movements of the long-leading composite index

CHART 9–1
Three Leading Indexes

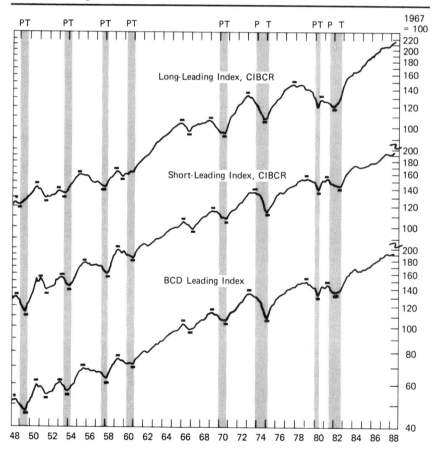

Shaded areas are business cycle recessions, from peak (P) to trough (T). BCD, *Business Conditions Digest.*

Source: Center for International Business Cycle Research (CIBCR), August 1988.

TABLE 9-2
Lead/Lag Record of CIBCR Long-Leading and Short-Leading Indexes and BCD Leading Index

Business Cycle		Leads at Peaks			Leads at Troughs			Long Leading vs. Short Leading		Long Leading vs. BCD Leading		Short Leading vs. BCD Leading	
P	T	Long Leading	Short Leading	BCD Leading	Long Leading	Short Leading	BCD Leading	P	T	P	T	P	T
11/48	10/49	-7	-5	-10	-13	-4	-4	-2	-9	+3	-9	+5	0
7/53	5/54	-8	-3	-4	-11	-4	-6	-6	-7	-4	-5	+1	+2
8/57	4/58	-27	-21	-23	-5	0	-2	-2	-5	-4	-3	+2	+2
4/60	2/61	-13	-11	-11	-15	-2	-2	0	-13	-2	-13	0	0
12/69	11/70	-10	-7	-8	-4	-1	-1	-3	-3	-2	-3	+1	0
11/73	3/75	-10	-4	-8	-5	-2	-1	-6	-3	-2	-4	+4	0
1/80	7/80	-26	-10	-10	-2	-2	-2	-16	0	-16	0	0	-1
7/81	11/82	-10	-3	-3	-10	-5	-8	-7	-5	-7	-2	0	+3
Mean													
P		-14	-8	-10				-6		-4		+2	
T					-8	-2	-3		-6		-5		+1

62

TABLE 9-2—Continued

Business Cycle	Leads at Peaks			Leads at Troughs			Long Leading vs. Short Leading		Long Leading vs. BCD Leading		Short Leading vs. BCD Leading	
P T	Long Leading	Short Leading	BCD Leading	Long Leading	Short Leading	BCD Leading	P	T	P	T	P	T
Standard deviation												
P	7	6	6				4		5		2	
T				4	2	2		4		4		1
Percentage leads												
P	100	100	100				100		88		0	
T				100	88	100		88		88		12
Extra cycles												
P dates	8/50	1/51	8/50	7/51	8/51	8/51						
	1/66	3/66	3/66	10/66	4/67	12/66						
T dates												

Abbreviations: CIBCR, Center for International Business Cycle Research; BCD, *Business Conditions Digest*; P, peak; T, trough.

TABLE 9-3
Long-Leading Index Forecasts and Other Forecasts of Real GNP, 1962–88[1]

		Year-to-Year Percentage Change, Real GNP				Forecast Errors		
	Long-Leading Growth Rate, Preceding (August) (1)	Forecast, Long Leading (August) (2)	Forecast, Economic Report (January) (3)	Forecast, Economists Consensus (November) (4)	Actual (5)	Long Leading (August) (6)	Economic Report (January) (7)	Economists Consensus (November) (8)
1961–62	11.9	5.5	8.0	na	5.3	0.2	2.7	na
1962–63	7.5	4.4	3.5	na	3.8	0.6	-0.3	na
1963–64	10.7	5.2	5.0	na	4.7	0.5	0.3	na
1964–65	8.3	4.6	4.0	na	5.4	-0.8	-1.4	na
1965–66	8.2	4.6	5.0	na	5.4	-0.8	-0.4	na
1966–67	-8.4	0.1	4.0	na	2.5	-2.4	1.5	na
1967–68	5.4	3.8	4.3	na	5.0	-1.2	-0.7	na
1968–69	4.5	3.6	3.5	3.3	2.8	0.8	0.7	0.5
1969–70	-6.5	0.6	1.3	1.1	-0.4	1.0	1.7	1.5
1970–71	-3.3	1.5	4.5	2.8	2.7	-1.2	1.8	0.1
1971–72	17.2	7.0	6.0	5.5	6.5	0.5	-0.5	-1.0
1972–73	10.1	5.1	6.8	6.1	5.9	-0.8	0.9	0.2
1973–74	-5.4	0.9	1.0	1.1	-2.2	3.1	3.2	3.3
1974–75	-15.7	-1.8	-3.0	-0.8	-2.0	0.2	-1.0	1.2
1975–76	16.0	6.6	6.2	5.9	6.2	0.4	0.0	-0.3
1976–77	10.8	5.2	5.2	5.0	4.9	0.3	0.3	0.1
1977–78	7.5	4.4	4.8	4.3	3.9	0.5	0.9	0.4
1978–79	-0.4	2.3	3.4	2.4	2.3	0.0	1.1	0.1
1979–80	-4.8	1.1	-0.1	-1.3	-0.2	1.3	0.1	-1.1
1980–81	-2.9	1.6	1.5	1.2	1.9	-0.3	-0.4	-0.7

TABLE 9-3—Continued

	Year-to-Year Percentage Change, Real GNP					Forecast Errors		
	Long-Leading Growth Rate, Preceding (August) (1)	Forecast, Long Leading (August) (2)	Forecast, Economic Report (January) (3)	Forecast, Economists Consensus (November) (4)	Actual (5)	Long Leading (August) (6)	Economic Report (January) (7)	Economists Consensus (November) (8)
1981–82	−3.5	1.4	0.9	0.5	−1.8	3.2	2.7	2.3
1982–83	6.4	4.1	1.7	2.4	3.3	0.8	−1.6	−0.9
1983–84	20.0	7.7	5.3	5.2	6.8	0.9	−1.5	−1.6
1984–85	4.1	3.5	3.7	3.4	2.3	1.2	1.4	1.1
1985–86	12.0	5.6	3.4	2.9	2.5	3.1	0.9	0.4
1986–87	7.8	4.4	2.7	2.5	2.9	1.5	0.2	0.4
1987–88	4.5	3.6	2.9	2.2	3.8	−0.2	−0.9	−1.4
		Correlation (RSQ), Forecast and Actual Change				Mean Absolute Error		
1962–76	—	0.80	0.78	na	—	1.0	1.1	na
1977–88	—	0.73	0.68	0.74	—	1.1	1.0	0.9

ᵃThe long-leading index forecasts (column 2) are based on the six-month smoothed growth rate for the preceding August (column 1) using a regression fitted to the actual data for the first 15 years, 1962–76 (column 5). Economic Report forecasts (column 3) are published in the *Economic Report of the President* in January of the year forecasted. Economists' consensus forecasts (column 4) are from the ASA-NBER survey of about 40 economists taken in November preceding the year forecast and published in December. The actual figures (column 5) are from the first official estimates published by the Department of Commerce in January following the forecast year (i.e., subsequent revisions are ignored). Abbreviations: GNP, gross national product; na, not available; ASA-NBER, American Statistical Association and National Bureau of Economic Research.

from 1948–87. It also shows the movements of a composite based on 11 short leaders. Five of the eleven are currently components of the Commerce Department index. The other six are among those recommended in this report for inclusion in a revised leading composite index. The long-leading composite leads the short-leading index by six months at both business cycle peaks and troughs. Used together, the long- and short-leading indexes help to interpret and confirm each other's movements.

The U.S. battery of economic indicators does not presently include a long-leading composite index. Economic forecasters naturally have a keen interest in the longest of leaders, and the long-leading index gives them another forecasting tool. Tests we have made of its ability to forecast yearly changes in real GNP suggest that it has considerable capacity in this respect (Table 9-3).[2] In addition, the short- and long-leading indexes supplement one another when a new trend appears in one index and is either confirmed or not by movements in the other index.

---

[2]See G. H. Moore, "A New Look at the Leading Indicators," University of Michigan Economic and Social Outlook Conference, November 1987, *The Economic Outlook for 1988*, Ann Arbor, Mich.

CHAPTER 10

PROMPTLY AVAILABLE ECONOMIC INDICATORS

Geoffrey H. Moore and John P. Cullity

INTRODUCTION

Prompt availability is an obvious requirement of a good economic indicator. For forecasting and decision making a series that is current deservedly commands attention; one that is stale is apt to be disregarded. This chapter describes an effort to construct more promptly available monthly economic indexes for the United States. Section 2 describes the criterion adopted for the selection of promptly available leading and coinciding indicators. It also compares the cyclical timing of these indicators with those used in the Commerce Department's composite indexes. Section 3 shows the behavior of the new promptly available composite indexes and compares them with the Commerce series. It also examines the usefulness of the new series for the CIBCR sequential signals of recession and recovery. Section 4 summarizes the main findings.

SELECTION OF INDICATORS

After surveying the available data, we defined a promptly available indicator as a statistic for which the data for a given month are released within the first seven days of the following month. Using this criterion, Table 10-1 provides the schedule of release dates for 12 leading indicators

TABLE 10-1
Release Schedules of Promptly Available Leading and Coincident Indicators

	Type of Monthly Figure*	Release Date in Following Month	Release Date for November 1987 data
Leading Indicators			
Marginal employment adjustments			
Average workweek, manufacturing (M)**	1	1st Friday	Dec. 4
Layoff rate, under five weeks (M)	1	1st Friday	Dec. 4
Initial claims, unemployment insurance (W)**	3	1st Thurs.	Dec. 3
Capital investment commitments			
Net business formation, CIBCR (W)	3	1st Wed. or Mon.	Dec. 7
Real estate loans, deflated, growth rate (W)	3	1st Monday	Nov. 30
Inventory investment and purchasing			
Vendor performance, NAPM survey (M)	1	1st Monday	Nov. 30
Inventory change, NAPM survey (M)	1	1st Monday	Nov. 30
Industrial materials prices, growth rate (D)	2	1st day	Dec. 1
Profitability			
Stock price index, S&P 500 (D)**	2	1st day	Dec. 1
Large business failures (W)	3	1st Monday	Dec. 7
Money and credit			
Broad money supply (M2), deflated (W)**	3	1st Monday	Dec. 4
Long-term bond prices, Dow Jones (D)	2	1st day	Dec. 1
Coincident Indicators			
Employee hours, nonfarm (M)	1	1st Friday	Dec. 4
Production survey, NAPM (M)	1	1st Monday	Nov. 30
Business Week production index (W)	3	1st Monday	Dec. 7

*Type of monthly figures: 1, survey week; 2, monthly average of daily figures; 3, four- or five-week average when available, otherwise, average of second and third week of the month.
**Included in Commerce Department's leading index.
Abbreviations: M, monthly; W, weekly; D, daily; CIBCR, Center for International Business Cycle Research; NAPM, National Association of Purchasing Management.

and 3 coincident indicators. Four of the leading series shown are, with some modifications, currently used in the Commerce Department's leading composite index. They are the average workweek in manufacturing, initial claims for unemployment insurance, the S&P 500 stock price index, and the money supply (M2), deflated. The other leading indicators in the table have been carefully studied, and some could serve as substitutes for or additions to the components of the Commerce index.

The 12 leading series obviously have much better currency than most of the components in the Commerce leading index. A leading index constructed with these promptly available components for November 1987 could have been released as early as December 7, 1987. The Commerce leading index for November was released December 29. Hence, the promptly available index would provide economists, policymakers, and the general public with "up-to-date" information about economic prospects some three weeks before the well-known leader. Furthermore, all of the proposed components are available early in the month. This constitutes an advantage over other indexes that are subject to revision because some components are not available when the index is first released. This often causes a significant revision of the index in the following month.

Similarly, the November 1987 figures for the three promptly available coincident indicators listed in Table 10-1 were released by December 7. None of these three are presently included in the Commerce coincident index, although we believe that employee-hours would be a desirable substitute for nonfarm employment in that index. Only three of the four components of the existing Commerce index are available when the index is first released toward the end of the month, and this produces revisions of the index the next month. This problem could be avoided by the use of the three promptly available indicators and setting the release date at the end of the first week of the following month, about three weeks before the present release date.

The average leads of each of the 12 promptly available leading indicators are shown in Table 10-2. For the group as a whole the average leads at business cycle peaks and troughs are 12 and 3 months, respectively. At both peaks and troughs, the lead is about eight months on average. These average leads are identical with those of the 11 components of the Commerce leading index.

Table 10-3 compares the distribution of leads and lags among the 12

TABLE 10-2
Average Leads at Business Cycle Turning Points, 1948–82: Twelve Promptly Available Leading Indicators

	Average Lead (−) or Lag (+), in Months		
	P	T	P&T
Marginal Employment Adjustments			
Average workweek, manufacturing*	−10	−2	−6
Layoff rate, under five weeks	−10	−2	−6
Initial claims, unemployment insurance*	−9	−1	−5
Capital Investment Commitments			
Net business formation (CIBCR)	−9	−2	−6
Real estate loans, deflated, growth rate	−11	−1	−6
Inventory Investment and Purchasing			
Vendor performance, NAPM survey	−10	−5	−7
Inventory change, NAPM survey	−8	−2	−5
Industrial materials prices, growth rate	−8	−2	−6
Profitability			
Stock price index, S&P 500*	−9	−5	−7
Large business failures, Dun & Brad-street	−18	−1	−9
Money and Credit			
Broad money supply (M2), deflated*	−17	−6	−11
Long-term bond prices, Dow Jones	−27	−7	−17
Average, 12 indicators	−12	−3	−8

*Included in Commerce Department's leading index.
Abbreviations: P, peaks; T, troughs; CIBCR, Center for International Business Cycle Research; NAPM, National Association of Purchasing Management.

promptly available leading indicators with those of the 11 components of the BCD leading index. The turns in the promptly available group led the business cycle turns about 73 percent of the time. This is a fairly good performance, although not quite as good as that of the 11 components of the Commerce index, which led 79 percent of the time. In terms of consistency in timing, the difference is mainly due to the fact that the

TABLE 10-3
Lead/Lag Records, 1948–82: BCD Leading Indicators and Promptly Available Leading Indicators

	Number of Observations		Percentage of Total	
	BCD Leading Indicators (1)	Promptly Available Leading Indicators (2)	BCD Leading Indicators (3)	Promptly Available Leading Indicators (4)
Timing at eight business cycle peaks				
Leads	81	79	92	82
Coincidences	2	3	2	3
Lags	0	1	0	1
No timing comparison	5	13	6	14
Total	88	96	100	100
Timing at eight business cycle troughs				
Leads	59	62	67	65
Coincidences	14	13	16	14
Lags	10	8	11	8
No timing comparison	5	13	6	14
Total	88	96	100	100
Timing at peaks and troughs				
Leads	140	141	79	73
Coincidences	16	16	9	8
Lags	10	9	6	5
No timing comparison	10	26	6	14
Total	176	192	100	100

Abbreviation: BCD, *Business Conditions Digest.*

promptly available series skipped turns more often. In the next section, we find that this does not seriously affect the performance of a composite index based on the promptly available components.

We have also compared leads, coincidences, and lags among the three promptly available coincident indicators with those of the four components of the BCD coincident index. From 1948–82, the turns in the three promptly available coincident series came within one month

TABLE 10-4

Lead/Lag Record: BCD Coincident Indicators and Promptly Available Coincident Indicators, 1948–82

	Average Lead (−) or Lag (+), in months	Number of Timing Comparisons		Percentage within One Month
		Within One Month	Total	
Timing at Eight Business Cycle Peaks				
BCD coincident indicators				
Nonfarm employment (41)	+1	3	8	38
Personal income excluding transfer (51)	+1	5	7	71
Industrial production (47)	−2	3	8	38
Manufacturing and trade sales (57)	−3	3	8	38
Promptly available indicators				
Nonfarm employee-hours	0	4	8	50
Production survey, NAPM	0	6	8	75
Business Week production index	−2	4	8	50
Timing at Eight Business Cycle Troughs				
BCD coincident indicators				
Nonfarm employment (41)	+1	7	8	88
Personal income excluding transfer payments (51)	−1	4	7	57
Industrial production (47)	0	8	8	100
Manufacturing and trade sales (57)	−1	5	8	75
Promptly available indicators				
Nonfarm employee-hours	0	6	8	75
Production survey, NAPM	0	6	8	75
Business Week production index	−1	6	8	75
Timing at Peaks and Troughs				
Four BCD coincident indicators	0	38	62	61
Three promptly available coincident indicators	−1	32	48	67

Abbreviations: BCD, *Business Conditions Digest*; NAPM, National Association of Purchasing Management.

of the business cycle peak and trough dates 67 percent of the time. The comparable statistic for the four components of the BCD index was 61 percent (Table 10-4).

COMPOSITE INDEXES

Using the traditional methodology, we have constructed promptly available leading and coincident composite indexes for the United States. The components of these indexes, as noted above, are statistics for which the data for a given month are released within the first seven days of the following month. Table 10-5 and Chart 10-1 provide comparisons between the new leading composite index and the Commerce leading index. We find that the new index led all of the 16 business cycle peaks and troughs during the 34-year period from 1948–82. Its average lead was nine months at peaks, four months at troughs, and six months at peaks and troughs. These average leads are virtually the same as those of the Commerce leading index. The leads at individual turns are also closely correlated.

Chart 10-1 shows the movements of the two indexes from 1948 to the present, together with the dates of business cycle recessions and recoveries. It would be very difficult for even the most serious student of economic indicators to determine which was the Commerce series and which the newly constructed index in the absence of the labels.

Table 10-6 and Chart 10-2 compare the new promptly available coincident composite index with the Commerce coincident index. Both indexes tended to lead business cycle peaks before 1970. Since then, the peaks in both indexes have been virtually coincident with business cycle peaks. At cyclical lows, the promptly available index led at three of the four troughs before 1970 but has been coincident since then. As Chart 10-2 shows, the monthly movements of the two indexes are very closely related. The promptly available index is somewhat more erratic, mainly because the employee-hours series is more erratic than the number employed.

In 1980, the CIBCR began developing a system of "sequential signals of recession and recovery" based on growth rates in the Commerce Department's leading and coincident indexes. The first signal of

TABLE 10-5
Lead/Lag Record of Two Leading Indexes

	Peak and Trough Dates						Lead (−) or Lag (+), in months					
Business Cycle		Promptly Available Leading Index		Commerce Leading Index		Promptly Available vs. Business Cycle		Commerce vs. Business Cycle		Promptly Available vs. Commerce		
P	T	P	T	P	T	P	T	P	T	P	T
11/48	10/49	6/48	6/49	1/48	6/49	−5	−4	−10	−4	+5	0
7/53	5/54	3/53	12/53	3/53	11/53	−4	−5	−4	−6	0	+1
8/57	4/58	7/55	11/57	9/55	2/58	−25	−5	−23	−2	−2	−3
4/60	2/61	7/59	12/60	5/59	12/60	−9	−2	−11	−2	+2	0
12/69	11/70	5/69	7/70	4/69	10/70	−7	−4	−8	−1	+1	−3
11/73	3/75	7/73	1/75	3/73	2/75	−4	−2	−8	−1	+4	−1
1/80	7/80	9/78	6/80	3/79	5/80	−16	−1	−10	−2	−6	+1
7/81	11/82	4/81	6/82	4/81	3/82	−3	−5	−3	−8	0	+3

TABLE 10-5—Continued

Peak and Trough Dates | Lead (−) or Lag (+), in months

	Business Cycle		Promptly Available Leading Index		Commerce Leading Index		Promptly Available vs. Business Cycle		Commerce vs. Business Cycle		Promptly Available vs. Commerce	
	P	T	P	T	P	T	P	T	P	T	P	T
Extra cycles	8/50	3/66	8/50	11/51	8/50	8/51						
			3/66	12/66	3/66	12/66						
Average												
P, T							−9	−4	−10	−3	0	0
P & T							−6		−6		0	
Standard deviation												
P, T							8.1	1.6	6.1	2.5	3.2	1.9
P & T							6.3		5.6		2.7	
Correlation (r)												
P, T											+.59	+.90
P & T											+.89	

Abbreviations: P, peak; T, trough.

recession (P1) occurs when the six-month smoothed growth rate in the leading index first declines below 2.3 percent. The second signal requires the leading index growth rate to fall below –1.0 percent and the coincident index rate to fall below 2.3 percent. The third signal is set off when the leading rate is below zero and the coincident below –1.0 percent. Tests of the signals with data for 1951–81 showed the signals would provide useful information on the state of the business cycle. Chart 10-1B shows the six-month smoothed growth rate in the promptly available index and in the Commerce leader. We have compared the dates when the new index and the Commerce index went through the P1 signal. The promptly available signal was triggered before six of the seven recessions and coincided on one occasion. The average lead was seven months

CHART 10–1

Promptly Available Leading Index (Center for International Business Cycle Research, CIBCR) and Commerce Department's Leading Index (*Business Conditions Digest*, BCD), 1948–88

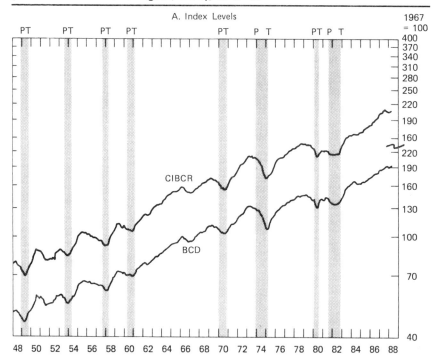

Shaded areas are business cycle recessions, from peak (P) to trough (T).

before the business cycle peaks. This record is virtually the same as that registered by the growth rates in the Commerce series. We also examined the behavior of the two series in triggering the first signal of recovery (i.e., T1). This signal is set off when the six-month smoothed rate of change in the leading composite first goes above +1.0 percent. The promptly available leading index signaled the eight recoveries with an average lag of one month, about a month later than the Commerce index did. This difference would be largely offset by the fact that the new index would be available about three weeks earlier.

SUMMARY

Our main findings are as follows:

1. A comprehensive set of leading and coincident indicators for the United States is available within seven days after the start of the

CHART 10–1—*continued*

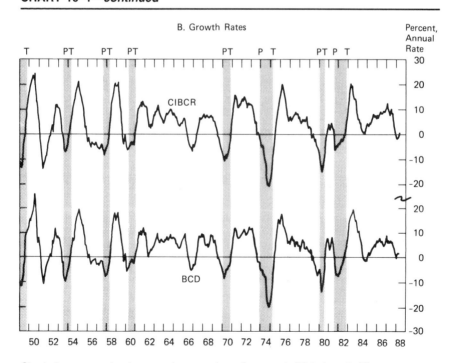

Shaded areas are business cycle recessions, from peak (P) to trough (T).

TABLE 10-6
Lead/Lag Record of Two Coincident Indexes

Business Cycle		Promptly Available Coincident Index		Commerce Coincident Index		Promptly Available vs. Business Cycle		Commerce vs. Business Cycle		Promptly Available vs. Commerce	
P	T	P	T	P	T	P	T	P	T	P	T
11/48	10/49	7/48	6/49	10/48	10/49	−4	−4	−1	0	−3	−4
7/53	5/54	7/53	2/54	5/53	8/54	0	−3	−2	+3	+2	−6
8/57	4/58	2/57	4/58	2/57	4/58	−6	0	−6	0	0	0
4/60	2/61	1/60	1/61	1/60	2/61	−3	−1	−3	0	0	−1
12/69	11/70	9/69	11/70	10/69	11/70	−3	0	−2	0	−1	0
11/73	3/75	11/73	3/75	11/73	3/75	0	0	0	0	0	0
1/80	7/80	2/80	7/80	1/80	7/80	+1	0	0	0	+1	0
7/81	11/82	5/81	11/82	7/81	11/82	−2	0	0	+1	−2	−1

TABLE 10-6—Continued

	Business Cycle		Promptly Available Coincident Index		Commerce Coincident Index		Promptly Available vs. Business Cycle		Commerce vs. Business Cycle		Promptly Available vs. Commerce	
	P	T	P	T	P	T	P	T	P	T	P	T
Average												
P, T							-2	-1	-2	0	0	-2
P & T							-2		-1		-1	
Standard deviation												
P, T							2.4	1.6	2.1	1.0	1.5	2.1
P & T							2.0		1.9		1.9	
Correlation (r)												
P, T											+.38	+.33
P & T											+.34	

Abbreviations: P, peak; T, trough.

CHART 10–2

Promptly Available Coincident Index (Center for International Business Cycle Research, CIBCR) and Commerce Department's Coincident Index (*Business Conditions Digest,* BCD), 1948–88

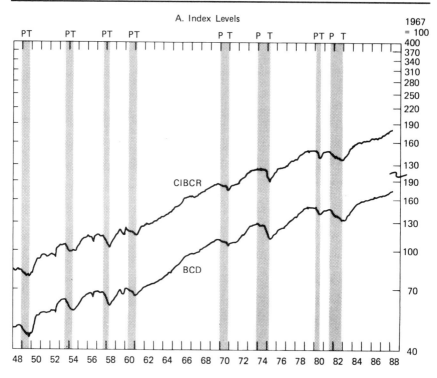

Shaded areas are business cycle recessions, from peak (P) to trough (T).

month, pertaining to activity during the previous month.

2. Composite indexes constructed from these indicators closely resemble those published by the Department of Commerce about three weeks later.

3. The new promptly available leading and coincident indexes are less subject to revision, because all of their components are available when the indexes are first compiled.

4. Initial signals of recession based on growth rates in the new leading index led the onset of recession by an average of seven months but lagged recoveries on average by one month.

CHART 10–2—*continued*

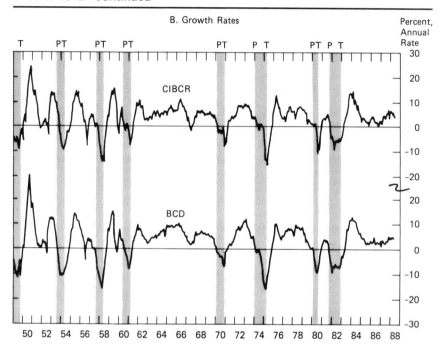

B. Growth Rates

Shaded areas are business cycle recessions, from peak (P) to trough (T).

CHAPTER 11

A MONTHLY INDEX
OF FINAL SALES

Geoffrey H. Moore

Two features of the coincident indicator, manufacturing and trade sales in 1982 dollars (BCD series 57), prompted our attempt to develop an alternative. One is that BCD series 57 for the preceding month is not available at the time (late in the following month) when the composite indexes are compiled. Hence, the initially reported coincident index includes only three components rather than four, and this leads to revisions in the following month. An index based on three components is not comparable with one based on four. The second deficiency is that BCD series 57 counts some types of manufactured goods more than once. Some are sold to other manufacturers, some to wholesalers, some to retailers, before they reach the final users. There is also duplication in the sales by wholesalers to retailers and then by retailers to consumers. As a result, manufacturing activity gets a very heavy weight (about half) in the total sales of manufacturers, wholesalers, and retailers.

In an effort to overcome these deficiencies, various combinations of the list of possible components shown in Table 11-1 have been considered. Most of these series are released initially in terms of current dollars, with data in 1982 dollars published subsequently, if at all. Hence, the notes to Table 11-1 propose various ways of obtaining a deflated series more promptly. These deflators could either be used to obtain a preliminary estimate that would later be revised or they might be used throughout the series, thus avoiding revisions and making the initial figures comparable with the later ones.

TABLE 11-1
Monthly Series Considered for Index of Final Sales

	Release Date for July 1988 Figures		
	In Current Dollars	In 1982 Dollars	Initial Year Covered
1. Retail sales (BCD series 54, 59)[1]	Aug 11	Aug 23	1947
2. Personal consumption expenditures[2]	Aug 26	Aug 26	1959*
3. Manufacturers shipments, capital goods industries[3]	Aug 23	Aug 26	1959
4. Manufacturers shipments, nondefense capital goods[3]	Aug 23	Aug 23	1958
5. Machinery and equipment sales[3]	Aug 23	Aug 23	
6. Machinery and equipment sales and business construction expenditures (BCD series 69)	Sept 1	na	1953
7. New one-family homes sold[4]	Aug 29	Aug 29	1963
8. Residential construction put-in-place	Sept 1		1947
9. Nonresidential construction put-in-place	Sept 1		1947
10. Merchandise trade balance[5]	Sept 14	na	1947

[1]Assumes CPI-commodities is used as deflator (release date August 23).
[2]Assumes CPI-total is used as deflator (release date August 23).
*Quarterly data are available back to 1947.
[3]Assumes these data are in the Advance Report on Durable Goods Shipments and can be deflated by the producer price index for producer finished goods (release date August 12).
[4]Reported number of houses sold is multiplied by the 1982 average price.
[5]Quantity indexes for imports and exports can be multiplied by 1982 values.
Abbreviation: na, not available.

One of the aggregates constructed from four of the series in Table 11-1 (i.e., series 1, 3, 7, and 9) did not prove to be a satisfactory coincident indicator (see Chart 11-1). It did not decline significantly during the 1969–70 recession and it led by four to eight months at three of the four peaks covered. In this respect it shows the same tendency to lead as manufacturing and trade sales, which has led at six of the eight peaks since 1948. Moreover, the inclusion of construction figures and new house sales would mean the aggregate could not be compiled in time for the release of the BCD indexes (which was August 30 for the July 1988 figures).

In view of these problems, we have compiled two additional aggregates covering sales of consumer goods and capital goods (including

CHART 11–1
Comprehensive Sales Measures

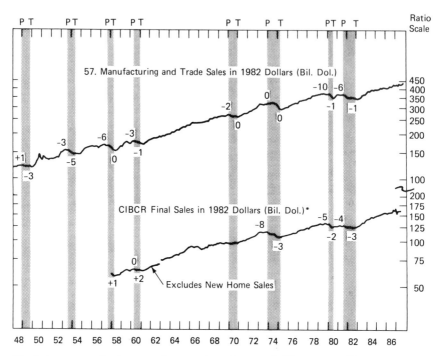

Shaded areas are business cycle recessions, from peak (P) to trough (T).
*Includes retail sales, capital goods sales, and nonresidential construction put in place.
CIBCR, Center for International Business Cycle Research.

defense). One aggregate includes retail sales, whereas the other includes personal consumption expenditures (series 1 and 2 in Table 11-1, respectively). The latter gives much broader coverage of services than does retail sales and, hence, is more stable. Services account for about half of personal consumption expenditures, whereas virtually the only types of retail stores that sell services directly are eating and drinking places and gasoline service stations, which account for about one-sixth of total retail sales. Hence, the annual total for consumption expenditures and capital goods sales is now about 3,000 billion in 1982 dollars, whereas for retail sales and capital goods sales it is about 1,800 billion 1982 dollars. The remaining 40 percent is the services component of consumption expenditures, a large portion of which is for housing.

One can see from Chart 11-2, however, that consumption expenditures and capital goods sales does not qualify as a coincident indicator, because it declines in only two of the five recessions since 1959. Retail sales and capital goods sales, however, perform well (Chart 11-3). This series has therefore been extended back to 1948, using the FRB index of production of business equipment and defense capital goods as a proxy for capital goods sales. Table 11-2 compares the leads

TABLE 11-2
Lead/Lag Record of Two Aggregate Sales Series

| Business Cycle Chronology | | Lead (−) or Lag (+), in months | | | |
| | | Manufacturing and Trade Sales in 1982 $ | | Retail and Capital Goods Sales in 1982 $ | |
P	T	P	T	P	T
11/48		+1		ntc	
	10/49		−3		ntc
7/53		−3		−4	
	5/54		−5		−4
8/57		−6		0	
	4/58		0		+1
4/60		−3		0	
	2/61		−1		0
12/69		−2		−2	
	11/70		0		0
11/73		0		0	
	3/75		0		−3
1/80		−10		−5	
	7/80		−1		−2
7/81		−6		+1	
	11/82		−1		−3
Mean					
P, T		−4	−1	−1	−2
P&T		−2		−2	
Standard deviation					
P, T		3.4	1.7	2.1	1.8
P&T		2.9		2.0	
Percentage roughly coincident					
P, T		62	88	71	86
P&T		75		79	

Abbreviations: P, peak; T, trough; ntc, no timing comparison.

CHART 11–2

Personal Consumption Expenditures and Capital Goods Sales in 1982 Dollars

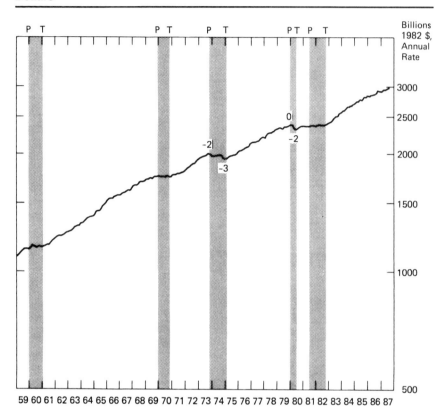

Shaded areas are business cycle recessions, from peak (P) to trough (T).

and lags of the new series with those of manufacturing and trade sales. The new series is a good coincident indicator, with an average lead of two months at business cycle peaks and troughs, modest variability in timing, and 79 percent of its turns occurring within three months of the business cycle turn. Its principal deficiency is its failure to conform to the 1948–49 recession.

In view of its unduplicated coverage, its timing record, and its availability when the BCD indexes are released, the series on retail sales and capital goods sales is a good candidate to replace manufacturing and trade sales in the coincident index. The suggested title for the series is "Final Sales of Consumer Goods and Capital Goods."

CHART 11–3

Deflated Retail Sales and Manufacturers' Shipments, Capital Goods Industries

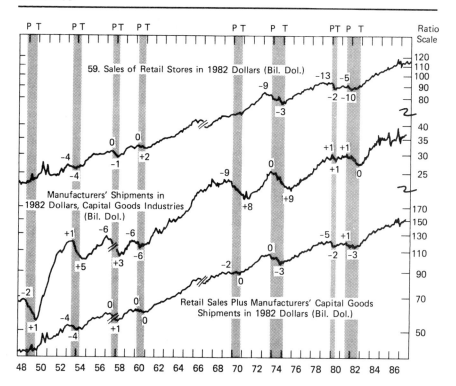

Prior to 1958, shipments data are industrial production for business and defense equipment adjusted to shipments level. Shaded areas are business cycle recessions, from peak (P) to trough (T).

CHAPTER 12

COMPREHENSIVE VERSUS CYCLE–SENSITIVE COINCIDENT INDICATORS

Geoffrey H. Moore

THE CONCEPTUAL ISSUE

One of the conceptual issues concerning the coincident indicators is whether they should be limited to, or at least aimed at, the most comprehensive measures of aggregate economic activity. Alternatively, should they focus upon those sectors of the economy that correspond most closely with business cycle fluctuations? There are arguments to be made on both sides of this question.

Let us first consider the kinds of economic variables that are relatively insensitive to cyclical movements or are even countercyclical. Agricultural output and employment is one sector that has long been considered relatively independent of business cycle movements. That is not true of all types of farming, and it may be less true now than in earlier times. Fertilization, cultivation, and irrigation practices have made harvests more dependent on economic considerations and less dependent on the weather. Moreover, the value of output or income from farming is more closely related to business cycles than is real output or income, because farm prices and earnings are affected by recessions. Another sector that is relatively independent involves the activities of government—state, local, and federal. Here again the situation is mixed. Some government expenditures, such as unemployment compensation payments, are very closely related to the state of the business cycle. Indeed, they have a countercyclical effect. Other types of expenditure, such as defense spending, may be little affected by business conditions, but sometimes, as when a war breaks out, have a dominant effect themselves. The 1961–69 business cycle expansion, for example, is usually considered to have lasted as long as it did mainly because of the effect of the Vietnam War on federal spending.

This type of argument can be extended to many of the private service industries, where employment has been growing rapidly for many years, without the up-and-down movement that is characteristic of employment in most goods-producing industries. Business cycle movements do become visible in service-sector employment, however, when one examines rates of growth in jobs or unemployment rates among those previously employed in services (see Chapter 13).

The advantage of focusing attention upon the cycle-sensitive sectors in choosing coincident indicators is that then the current economic condition becomes more clearly visible, and perhaps more promptly apparent, than it would be otherwise. On the other hand, this may be at the cost of exaggerating the amplitude of the cycle and possibly misrepresenting its timing. In fact, some downswings that appear in cycle-sensitive measures might not be evident in more comprehensive measures. Also, if there has been a secular rise in the relative importance of the less sensitive (or countercyclical) elements, the effect of this on the whole economy may not be fully reflected in the cycle-sensitive measures alone.

THE COMMERCE DEPARTMENT'S COINCIDENT INDICATORS

The existing set of four coincident indicators used in the Commerce Department's composite coincident index may be examined from this point of view. The four series are

1. Index of industrial production.
2. Real manufacturing and trade sales.
3. Real personal income less transfer payments.
4. Nonfarm employment.

The industrial production index concentrates on the nonfarm goods-producing sector, excluding private and public services as well as construction activity and agriculture. Manufacturing and trade sales include some services sold by retailers to consumers but gives much more weight to goods, because the same goods may be represented in sales by one manufacturer to another, manufacturers to wholesalers, and wholesalers to retailers. The exclusion of transfer payments from personal income removes both countercyclical sources of income (unemployment compensation) as well as relatively steady sources (social security benefits). This exclusion, of course, makes the indicator more sensitive to business cycles but less reflective of the trend toward greater stability in total income. The nonfarm employment series excludes agricultural employment, which has diminished in relative importance. Hence, this measure has tended to overstate the trend toward steadier total employment. Moreover, because the source of this series is the payroll reports by employers, persons with more than one job may get counted twice, and the prevalence of dual job-holding changes over the business cycle. One way to avoid this, and at the same time obtain a more cycle-sensitive measure as well as a more accurate measure of total labor input, is to use nonfarm employee-hours. This reflects changes in the prevalence of part-time work, changes in overtime, and so on.

ALTERNATIVE LISTS

The upshot is that the existing set of four coincident indicators has gone part of the way toward the cycle-sensitive option, but not all the way. Perhaps we can help to resolve the issue by listing two sets of monthly measures of aggregate economic activity, one that includes the most comprehensive available measures while the other includes only the cycle sensitive. The lists are shown in Table 12-1.

Within each of these lists there is some duplication. For example, in List B there are six measures of employment, differing both as to source and whether the measure pertains to number of persons (10) and (11), number of jobs (12) and (13), or number of hours paid for (14) and (15). In List B also there are several measures of output. The first two are components of the experimental index placed in List A, which is being developed by the FRB and includes measures of services as well as goods output. The other three output indexes are limited to goods production.

The series in each of these lists should receive careful study before a

TABLE 12-1
Two Lists of Monthly Measures of Aggregate Economic Activity

A. Comprehensive Aggregates

1. Total output, FRB (M)
2. Real final sales, CIBCR (M)
3. Real consumption expenditures (M)
4. Real personal income (M)
5. Total employment, household survey (M)

B. Cycle-Sensitive Aggregates

1. Private sector output, FRB (M)
2. Nonfarm private sector output, FRB (M)
3. Industrial production, FRB (M)*
4. *Business Week* production index (W)
5. NAPM production index (M)
6. Real manufacturing and trade sales (M)*
7. Real final sales, consumer and capital goods, CIBCR (M)
8. Real personal income excluding transfer payments (M)*
9. Real nonfarm personal income excluding transfer payments (M)
10. Civilian employment, household survey (M)
11. Civilian nonfarm employment, household survey (M)
12. Nonfarm employment, payroll survey (M)*
13. Nonfarm business employment, payroll survey (M)
14. Nonfarm employee-hours, payroll survey (M)
15. Nonfarm business employee-hours, payroll survey (M)

Abbreviations: FRB, Federal Reserve Board; M, monthly; W, weekly; NAPM, National Association of Purchasing Management; CIBCR, Center for International Business Cycle Research.
*Included in *Business Conditions Digest* coincident index.

final choice is made of series to include in a coincident index. Possibly several alternative indexes should be constructed and evaluated, based upon selections from one or the other or both lists. Other considerations must be taken into account, such as the promptness with which figures for the indicators are available. Regarding two of the series in the list, however, the case seems clear, namely, the substitution of nonfarm employee-hours for nonfarm employment and the substitution of final sales of consumer and capital goods for manufacturing and trade sales.

CHAPTER 13

NEW ECONOMIC INDICATORS FOR THE SERVICE INDUSTRIES

Geoffrey H. Moore and Allan P. Layton

INTRODUCTION

Although the service industries have become a dominant factor in the U.S. economy, they have not figured importantly in the Commerce Department's list of economic indicators. One reason for this is that many of the service industries have continued to grow during business cycle contractions as well as expansions. Indicators that skip recessions do not get a good rating as indicators and, hence, tend to be rejected. Many of the indicators that have been selected in the past, therefore, have pertained to manufacturing or construction activity, which are highly sensitive to business cycles.

It is important, however, that indicators be representative of the entire economy. Because the economy has become more service oriented, the list of indicators should reflect this. In some instances, more comprehensive data or data that give less dominant weight to manufacturing can be used. Hence, in the last section of this Chapter we recommend several indicators that would improve the coverage of services in the existing indexes.

The most effective way, we believe, to represent the service sectors in the indicator system is to analyze service industry data in terms of growth rates. The growth rates expose the cyclical fluctuations effectively and can be used to identify leading, coincident, and lagging indicators of service activity. Use of growth rates, however, means that the service indicators do not fit readily into the framework of the Commerce Department's list of indicators, which are largely expressed as levels. Hence, we propose that the service industry growth rate indicators be presented on a stand-alone basis, although, of course, they can and should be compared with growth rates in goods-producing industries and in the overall economy. The development of a new set of leading and coincident indicators for services, and their growth rates, was undertaken by CIBCR as a separate project, supported by the Coalition of Service Industries, and is reported in the next section.

NEW SERVICES INDICATORS BASED ON GROWTH RATES

As an example of the effectiveness of analyzing service industry data in terms of growth rates, consider Chart 13-1, which compares the growth of employment in services with that in goods-producing industries. Although total employment in the service industries has risen with scarcely any interruption since 1960, the growth rate in service industry employment is highly sensitive to the business cycle. It usually reaches a peak six months to a year before the business cycle peak and a trough at about the same time as the business cycle trough. In this respect it corresponds quite closely to the growth of employment in the goods-producing industries.

However, the swings in the latter are far wider and have remained at negative levels for many months in every recession, contrasting sharply with the service industries' growth rates. These differences, together with the growing importance of services as a source of jobs, have tended to reduce both the length and the depth of recessions.[1]

In order to pursue this type of analysis and develop service industry growth rate indicators, a separate study was undertaken by the CIBCR during 1988, supported by a grant from the Coalition of Service Industries. As a first step in the procedure we established a growth chronology for services, representing peaks and troughs in the growth of comprehensive measures of services output, income, sales, and employment.

---

[1]See G. H. Moore, "The Service Industries and the Business Cycle," *Business Economics,* April 1987, pp. 12–17.

CHART 13–1
**Growth Rate in Employment in the Service Industries and
Goods-Producing Industries**

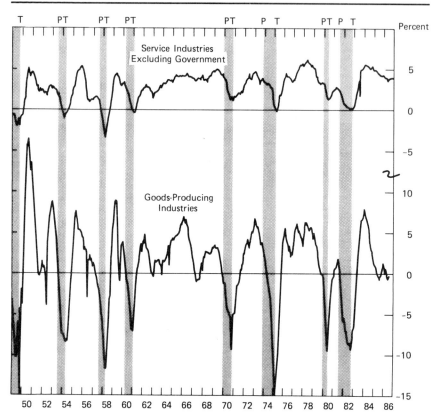

Note: Growth rates are annual rates based upon the ratio of the current month's employment
to the average level of employment during the previous 12 months, using seasonally
adjusted data. Shaded areas are business cycle recessions, from peak (P) to trough (T).

Each series was expressed in terms of its growth rate and the cyclical
highs and lows in growth were identified. The growth rate used here and
throughout the study was the six-month smoothed annual percentage rate
(or two-quarter smoothed rate in the case of quarterly data). It is based on
the ratio of the current month's (or quarter's) level to the average level
during the preceding 12 months (or four quarters) expressed as a compound annual rate.

The services growth chronology and the series used to identify it are displayed in Chart 13-2. From these series a coincident index was constructed using monthly (M) data as far back as available and quarterly (Q) data earlier. It should be noted that a new monthly output index for services, compiled by the FRB, was also used to obtain the chronology. However, since the FRB index is still considered experimental and not for current publication, it has not been used in the composite index. Hence, the four coincident indicators in the index are

Services employee-hours (M).

Services real labor income (M) (Q before 1965).

Services real output, GNP (Q).

Services real consumption expenditures (M) (Q before 1960).

The growth rate in the services coincident index, which also was used to help determine the services growth chronology, is shown in Chart 13-3, together with the growth rate in the Department of Commerce's coincident index based on four comprehensive measures of goods and services activity (nonfarm employment, industrial production, real personal income, and real manufacturing and trade sales). We find that the growth rates in services and in the overall economy are strikingly similar in their cyclical timing. However, the swings are far wider and deeper in the overall economy than in services.

To develop a set of leading indicators for the services sector, we examined a conceptually similar range of indicators that have proven effective for the overall economy. The following four series qualified as leading indicators of the services growth chronology:

Average workweek, services (M).

Commercial building contracts, floor space (M).

Stock price index, services (M).

Index of profit margins, services (M) (Q before 1977).

The growth rates in these four indicators match the services growth chronology well and lead the turning points rather consistently (see Chart 13-4 and Table 13-1).

CHART 13-2
Growth Rates in Coincident Indicators for Services

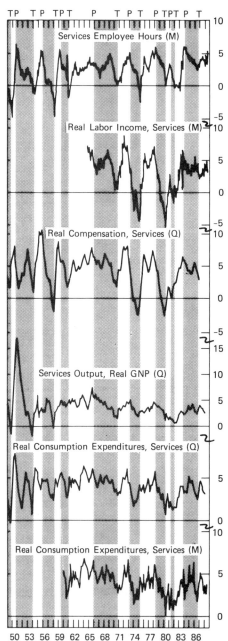

Shaded areas represent slowdowns in the services growth chronology. P, peak; T, trough; M, monthly; Q, quarterly; GNP, gross national product.

CHART 13–3

Growth Rates in Coincident Indexes for Services and Overall Economy

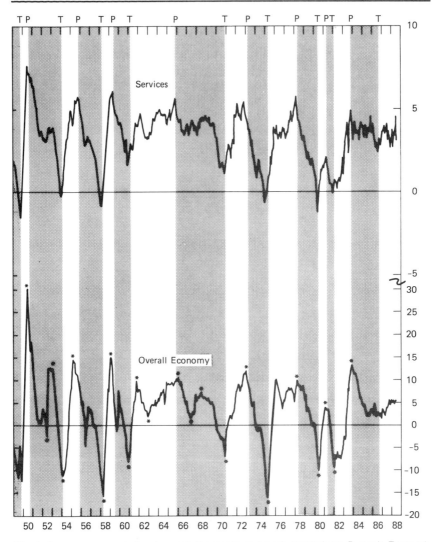

Shaded areas represent slowdowns in the services growth chronology. P, peak; T, trough.

Source: Center for International Business Cycle Research.

From these series a leading index was constructed, as displayed in Charts 13-5 and 13-6. Its growth rate led 14 of the 16 turns in the services growth chronology and was coincident twice (Table 13-2). On average, it

TABLE 13-1
Lead/Lag Record of Four Services Leading Indicators

Services Growth Chronology		Leads (−) and Lags (+) of Growth Rates, in months							
		Stock Price Index, Services		Average Work-week, Services		Index of Profit Margins, Services		Construction Contracts Commercial Buildings, Floor Space	
P	T	P	T	P	T	P	T	P	T
8/50	10/49	−6	ntc	+5	0	+3	+1	0	−13
11/55	2/54	−15	−8	−11	−22	−9	−3	−11	−2
6/59	4/58	−5	−4	−2	−6	−7	−2	−2	−6
11/65	3/61	−30	−13	−41	−2	−48	−10	+3	−16
3/73	11/70	−24	−6	−15	−7	−25	−9	−2	−1
4/78	4/75	−34	−7	ntc	0	−8	−8	+1	−1
4/81	5/80	+2	−27	−2	+2	−7	−1	−4	0
10/83	1/82	−5	+5	0	0	−11	+5	+1	0

TABLE 13-1—Continued

| | Services Growth Chronology | | Leads (−) and Lags (+) of Growth Rates, in months | | | | | | | |
| | | | Stock Price Index, Services | | Average Work-week, Services | | Index of Profit Margins, Services | | Construction Contracts Commercial Buildings, Floor Space | |
	P	T	P	T	P	T	P	T	P	T
Mean										
P, T			−15	−9	−9	−4	−14	−3	−2	−5
P&T			−12		−7		−9		−3	
Standard deviation										
P, T			12.4	8.9	14.2	7.0	14.7	4.9	4.0	6.0
P&T			11.3		11.0		12.2		5.3	
Percent leads										
P, T			88	86	71	50	88	75	50	75
P&T			87		60		81		63	

Abbreviations: P, peak; T, trough; ntc, no timing comparison.

CHART 13–4
Growth Rates of Leading Indicators of Services

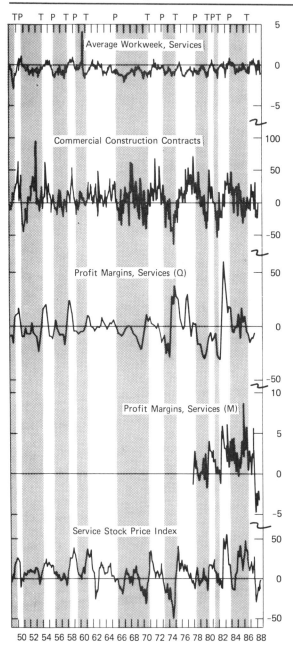

Shaded areas represent slowdowns in the services growth chronology. P, peak; T, trough; Q, quarterly; M, monthly.

led by nine months at all the turns. It also led the growth rate in the services coincident index by nine months on average. Compared with the leading index for the overall economy, as compiled by the Commerce Department, the services leading index growth rate has a similar configuration but a much smaller amplitude (Chart 13-7). As noted in the

CHART 13–5
Leading and Coincident Indexes for Services

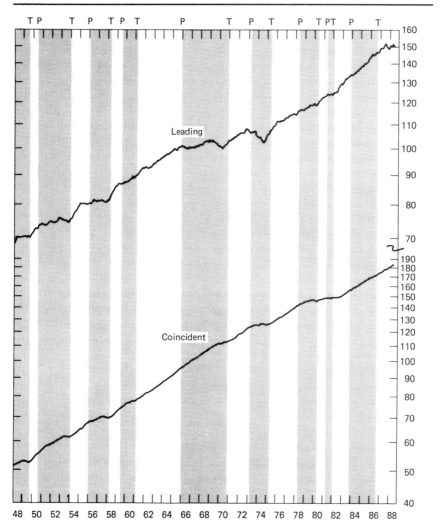

Shaded areas represent slowdowns in the services growth chronology. P, peak; T, trough.

TABLE 13-2
Lead/Lag Record of Services Coincident and Leading Indexes

Services Growth Chronology		Growth Rate, Coincident Index				Growth Rate, Leading Index			
		Dates		Lead/Lag (months)		Dates		Lead/Lag (months)	
P	T	P	T	P	T	P	T	P	T
8/50	10/49	8/50	10/49	0	0	6/50	10/49	-2	0
11/55	2/54	12/55	1/54	+1	-1	2/55	11/53	-9	-3
6/59	4/58	6/59	4/58	0	0	1/59	10/57	-5	-6
11/65	3/61	12/65	1/61	+1	-2	6/63	3/60	-29	-12
3/73	11/70	12/72	11/70	-3	0	3/71	5/70	-24	-6
4/78	4/75	4/78	1/75	0	-3	7/75	8/74	-33	-8
4/81	5/80	4/81	5/80	0	0	3/81	3/80	-1	-2
10/83	1/82	12/83	1/82	+2	0	5/83	1/82	-4	0

TABLE 13-2—Continued

Services Growth Chronology		Growth Rate, Coincident Index				Growth Rate, Leading Index			
		Dates		Lead/Lag (months)		Dates		Lead/Lag (months)	
P	T	P	T	P	T	P	T	P	T
Mean									
P, T				0	−1			−13	−5
P&T					−1				−9
Standard deviation									
P, T				1.2	1.4			12.3	4.0
P&T					1.4				10.0
Percent leads									
P, T				12	50			100	75
P&T					31				88
Extra cycles		None				11/61	10/62		
						7/68	9/66		
						4/86	7/84		

Abbreviations: P, peaks; T, troughs.

introduction, the Commerce Department's leading index is heavily weighted by indicators representing goods-producing activity. Hence, the contrast in amplitudes may be reflecting the difference between goods and services.

CHART 13–6
Growth Rates in Leading and Coincident Indexes for Services

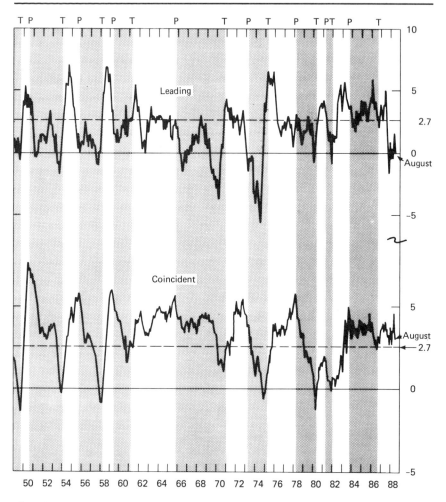

Growth rates are based on the ratio of the current month's index to the average index for the preceding 12 months, expressed as a compound annual rate. Shaded areas represent slowdowns in the service industries growth chronology. Horizontal dashed line is the growth rate, 1976–86, in the services output and in both indexes. P, peak; T, trough.

CHART 13-7   Growth Rates in Leading Indexes for Services Industries and the Entire Economy

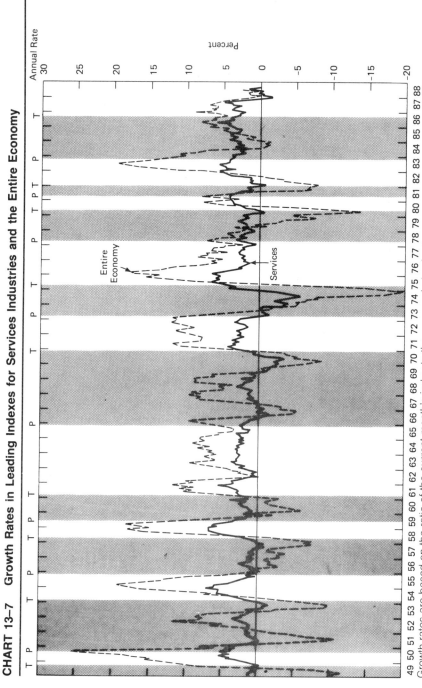

Growth rates are based on the ratio of the current month's index to the average index for the preceding 12 months, expressed as a compound annual rate. Shaded areas represent slowdowns in the service industries growth chronology. The leading index for the entire economy is published by the Department of Commerce. P, peaks, T, troughs.

We hope that with further research we may be able to improve the coverage and quality of the services indicators. The Dun & Bradstreet data on business starts and business failures in service industries warrant attention in this connection. Now that the statistical agencies are devoting more effort to reporting on the services sector, a broader collection of indicators in this field may become available. Some steps in this direction are discussed next.

IMPROVING SERVICES COVERAGE IN THE EXISTING LIST OF INDICATORS

Leading Indicators

One of the new series we have recommended as a leading indicator (Chapter 2), namely, net business formation, provides extensive coverage of services as well as goods-producing industries. Indeed, the number of new business enterprises in the service sector is a dominant factor in total business starts. Hence, the series on net business formation, based on business starts and failures as compiled by Dun & Bradstreet, Corp., will enhance the coverage of services in the leading index.

Coincident Indicators

A new series on retail sales and capital goods sales in 1982 dollars has been designed to replace manufacturing and trade sales in the coincident index. This will reduce the dominant weight of manufactured goods in the coincident index, because the aggregate of manufacturing and trade sales counts sales of manufactured goods more than once, as they are sold and resold among manufacturers, wholesalers, and retailers. In the new series on retail sales and capital goods sales, manufactured goods are counted only when they reach the final user. For further discussion, see Chapter 11.

Transportation services are not directly represented among the four coincident indicators presently included in the coincident index. Because the services provided by airlines, railroads, trucks, buses, subways, pipelines, ships, and so on are vitally important to the economy, we believe this situation should be remedied. The Commerce Department has recently constructed a freight traffic index that includes most forms of land-based freight but not sea-borne. We believe that further work needs to be done to include both ocean freight and passenger traffic. As a step in that direction, we have constructed an airline traffic index, which includes both cargo-miles and passenger-miles (Chart 13-8). A comprehensive monthly index of transportation output has recently been constructed by the FRB from 1977 to date (see Chart 13-9). It has promising qualifications as a coincident indicator, although we should like to see it extended back to earlier years and released promptly enough to be used in the initial release of the Commerce coincident index. In that

CHART 13–8
Index of Domestic Air Traffic

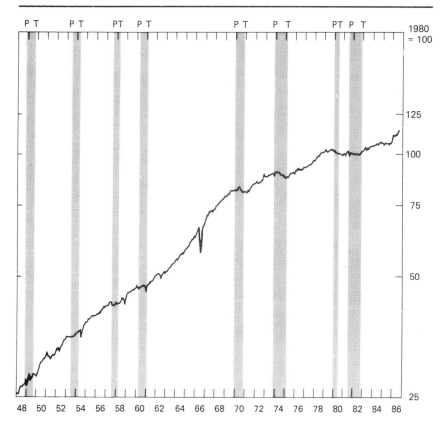

Index is based on seasonally adjusted data for domestic air passenger-miles and domestic air cargo ton-miles. Shaded areas are business cycle recessions, from peak (P) to trough (T).

CHART 13–9
Federal Reserve Board Index of Transportation Output, 1977–86

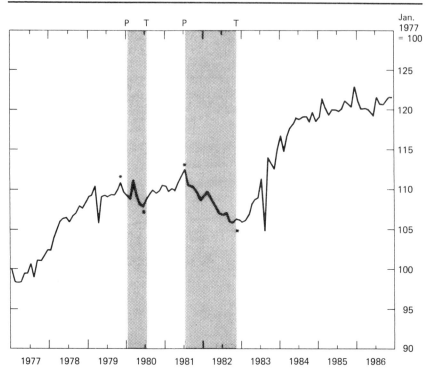

Shaded areas are business cycle recessions, from peak (P) to trough (T).

way it would supplement the presently used index of industrial production, covering an important class of services.

The FRB also has been developing a monthly index of goods and services output, with coverage similar to that of real GNP.[2] Although the new index is considered to be experimental, it too shows promise as a coincident indicator. Expressed in quarterly form, its growth rate corresponds quite closely to real GNP growth, although the discrepancy since the middle of 1986 is disturbing (see Chart 13-10). Also, the problem remains of how to obtain a reasonable monthly equivalent to the index before 1977.

---

[2]See Z. Kennessey, "Experimental Indexes of Service Production," 50th Anniversary Conference on Research in Income and Wealth, Washington, D.C., May 12–14, 1988.

CHART 13–10

Growth Rates in Real Gross National Product (GNP) and Federal Reserve Board (FRB) Index of Goods and Services Production, 1978–87

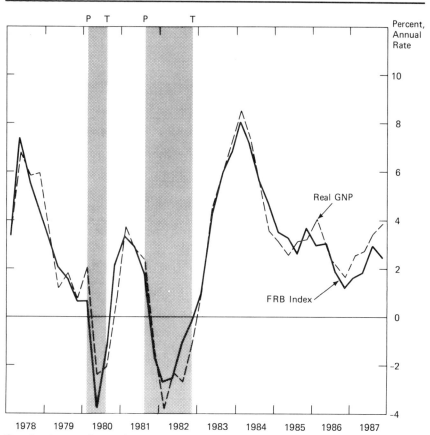

Growth rates are six-month smoothed rates, based on ratio of current quarter to average of the preceding four quarters, expressed as annual rate. FRB index is available monthly, but quarterly averages are used here. Shaded areas are business cycle recessions, from peak (P) to trough (T).

Source: Center for International Business Cycle Research, March 1988.

Although employment in the service industries has declined only briefly, if at all, in recessions, the slower growth rate during recession has regularly resulted in an increase in unemployment among those attached to the service industries. At our suggestion, the BLS has computed a new monthly series on the unemployment rate for the service industries as a whole, which can be compared with a similar rate for goods-producing industries (Chart 13-11). The rates pertain to job losers who identify the industry to which they were previously attached. Both rates conform closely to the business cycle, but the service industries rate is generally lower, especially in recessions. Although the rates do not qualify as coincident indicators because of their tendency to lead at peaks and lag or coincide at troughs, we do recommend that they be included in BCD, along with the total unemployment rate.

A better measure of labor input than the number of persons employed is the total number of hours they work. This is especially important in connection with the service industries because of the substantially shorter average workweek in this sector. In 1987, for example, the average workweek in services was about 33 hours, whereas in manufacturing it was 41 hours. This is largely because many more part-time workers are being employed in service establishments. In order to recog-

CHART 13–11

Unemployment Rates in Goods-Producing Industries and in Services-Producing Industries

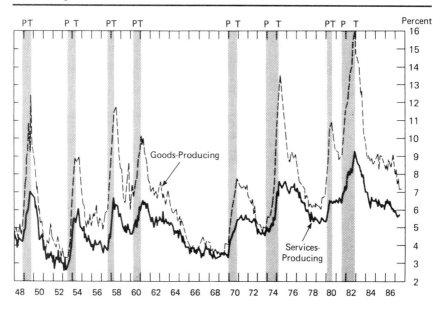

Data are seasonally adjusted. Shaded areas are business cycle recessions, from peak (P) to trough (T).

Source: Bureau of Labor Statistics.

nize this situation and at the same time include a more accurate measure of total labor input in the coincident index, we recommend that employee-hours in nonfarm establishments (BCD series 48) be substituted for the number of nonfarm employees, which is presently used in the index. In addition, it is a more sensitive economic indicator, because the average workweek component of total employee-hours fluctuates with the business cycle and usually leads movements in the number of persons employed.[3]

If all the above proposals were adopted, the coincident index would include four or five series, as follows:

Retail sales and capital goods sales, in 1982 dollars.

Index of transportation output
Industrial production index $\Big\}$ or Total goods and services output.

Nonfarm employee-hours.

Personal income less transfer payments, in 1982 dollars.

The result would be an index more representative of our goods and services economy than the existing index.

Lagging Indicators

The prices of services comprise a large and growing proportion of the consumer price index (CPI). Between December 1973 and December 1986 the relative importance of services in the CPI rose from 36.5 to 54.4 percent. Hence, the overall inflation rate is significantly influenced by the rate of inflation in services prices, now more than ever. We have found that the services inflation rate is a consistent lagging indicator with respect to business cycles (Chart 13-12 and Table 13-3). The lag probably reflects the fact that wages, an important cost element in services, also are a lagging indicator. Because it would be desirable to have services directly represented in the lagging index, we recommend that the growth rate of the service price index be included.

---

[3]One of the deficiencies in the employee-hours series is that occasionally it is affected by the occurrence of a major holiday in the survey week (week including the 12th of the month). This usually produces a sharp drop in the month affected and a recovery in the following month. We have recommended that the BLS modify its seasonal adjustment program to correct for these aberrations, and they are doing so.

CHART 13–12
Consumer Price Index for Services, Growth Rate

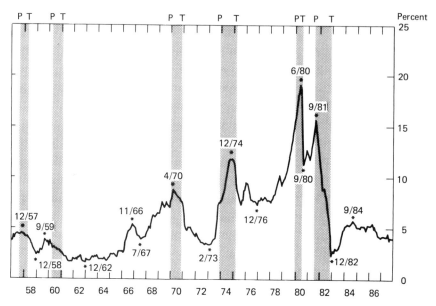

Shaded areas are business cycle recessions, from peak (P) to trough (T).

Diffusion Indexes

Still another method of achieving broader coverage of the service industries among economic indicators is to utilize diffusion indexes. Such
indexes measure an important dimension of business cycles—their scope.
Recessions would be of much less consequence if they affected only a
few industries, companies, or sectors of the economy. A diffusion index
tells us how widespread a recession is and whether it is widening or
narrowing. Several of the diffusion indexes now carried in BCD are
restricted to manufacturing. For example, the diffusion index for the
average workweek covers 20 manufacturing industries. Some years ago
the BLS constructed a similar index covering 186 nonfarm industries. We
suggest that this index be brought up to date and be considered as a
replacement for the manufacturing index. It would provide coverage of
the service industries and be a better measure of the real scope of cyclical

fluctuations, comparable with the existing diffusion index of nonfarm employment, which also covers 186 industries (recently extended to 349 industries). In addition, as noted in Chapter 1, we recommend that the presentation of diffusion indexes in BCD be simplified so that they would gain more attention.

TABLE 13-3
Lead/Lag Record of Consumer Price Index for Services, Growth Rate[1]

Business Cycle		Serivces Price Index, Growth Rate			
		Dates of		Lead (−) or Lag (+), in months	
P	T	P	T	P	T
8/57		12/57		+4	
	4/58		12/58		+8
4/60		9/59		−7	
	2/61		12/62		+22
12/69		4/70		+4	
	11/70		2/73		+27
11/73		12/74		+13	
	3/75		12/76		+21
1/80		6/80		+5	
	7/80		9/80		+2
7/81		9/81		+2	
	11/82		12/82		+1
Mean					
P, T				+4	+14
P&T				+8	
Median					
P, T				+4	+14
P&T				+4	
Percent lags					
P, T				83	100
P&T				92	
Extra cycles		11/66			
			7/67		
		9/84			

[1]The index is not available before 1956. The growth rate is the six-month smoothed percentage change at annual rate, based on seasonally adjusted data.
Abbreviations: P, peak; T, trough.

Source: Bureau of Labor Statistics.

CHAPTER 14

UNIT LABOR COST

Charlotte Boschan and Geoffrey H. Moore

One of the six components of the Commerce Department's lagging index is labor cost per unit of output in manufacturing as a percentage of trend. During the 1960s and 1970s when labor costs and prices were advancing rapidly, the removal of trend greatly improved the labor cost's performance as an indicator. Otherwise it rose through every recession. But between 1982 and 1984 unit labor cost declined, and since 1984 it has been nearly flat. Nevertheless, until 1987 the trend that was removed from the series continued to rise rapidly, with the result that the trend-adjusted series included in the lagging index declined sharply to levels never before reached in its entire history. Recently, at our suggestion, the trend has been revised to take care of this problem.

The CIBCR has developed a method of trend-fitting that makes better use of recent data in extrapolating trends, and the use of this method will, we believe, yield more reliable results. Nevertheless, this method still requires decisions on how frequently to revise the trend. An approach that avoids this problem is to convert the original data to growth rates and use the growth rate as the indicator. Because growth rates in unit labor costs, wage rates, and prices are widely used, the growth rate approach would provide useful information. However, cyclical swings in growth rates tend to lead those in the levels of the series from which they are derived, so the use of growth rates in unit labor costs might convert a lagging indicator into a leading indicator. In fact, that is not the case, and in view of the wide use of growth rates in price and cost analysis, we recommend that the six-month smoothed growth rate in unit labor cost in manufacturing be substituted for the trend-adjusted series in the lagging index. It

CHART 14–1

Two Measures of Growth Rate in Unit Labor Cost, Manufacturing

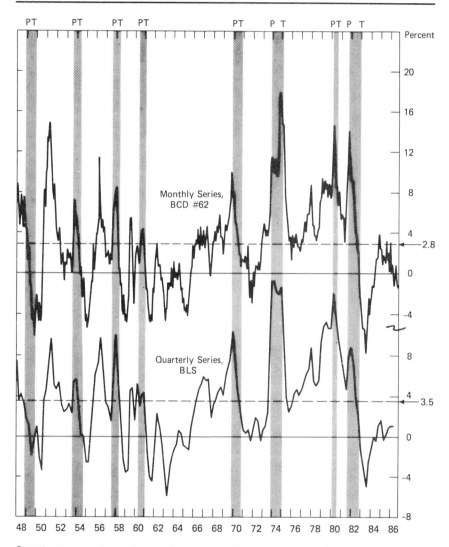

Growth rates are six-month smoothed rates and two-quarter smoothed rates, respectively. The horizontal dash lines are the average annual rate, 1948–86. Shaded areas are business cycle recessions, from peak (P) to trough (T). BCD, *Business Conditions Digest*; BLS, Bureau of Labor Statistics.

would be preferable to use a series with broader industrial coverage, but the only others available are quarterly rather than monthly (total nonfarm, nonfarm business, and nonfinancial corporations) and, hence, involve long publication delays.

In addition, we recommend a change in the method of deriving the monthly unit labor cost series for manufacturing. It is presently derived by using the FRB index of manufacturing production as the output variable. As a result, the monthly unit labor cost series is not the same as the quarterly series published by BLS, where the FRB output figures are adjusted to the annual levels of real income originating in manufacturing. This has an important effect on the trend. Real income originating has had a less rapid upward trend since 1947 than the FRB output series (see Chapter 5). Hence, the quarterly BLS unit labor cost rises more rapidly

CHART 14–2
A New Measure of Unit Labor Cost, Manufacturing: Growth Rate

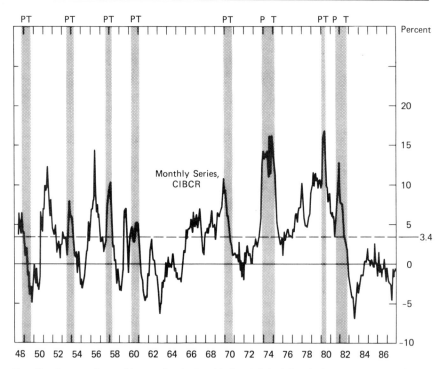

Growth rates are six-month smoothed rates. Horizontal dash line is the average annual rate, 1948–86. Shaded areas are business cycle recessions, from peak (P) to trough (T). CIBCR, Center for International Business Cycle Research.

than the existing monthly series. Between 1948 and 1986 the quarterly series rose at the average rate of 3.5 percent, whereas the monthly series rose at a 2.8 percent rate (see Chart 14-1). We have, therefore, derived a new monthly series on unit labor cost by adjusting the output figures to the annual levels of real output originating in manufacturing. An important test of the validity of this adjustment is that the price/unit labor cost ratio that it yields is more closely related to measures of profit margins (see Chapter 5). The growth rate in the new unit labor cost series is shown in Chart 14-2, and its lead/lag record is in Table 14-1. It lags quite consistently at business cycle peaks and troughs, and we, therefore, recommend it for the index of lagging indicators.

TABLE 14-1
Lead/Lag Record of Unit Labor Cost Growth Rate, Manufacturing

Business Cycle		Unit Labor Cost Growth Rate, Manufacturing		Lead (−) or Lag (+), in months, of Unit Labor Cost Growth Rate	
P	T	P	T	P	T
11/48		8/48		−3	
	10/49		11/49		+1
7/53		12/53		+5	
	5/54		3/55		+10
8/57		3/58		+7	
	4/58		4/59		+12
4/60		1/61		+9	
	2/61		4/63		+26
12/69		1/70		+1	
	11/70		1/72		+14
11/73		3/75		+16	
	3/75		2/76		+11
1/80		6/80		+5	
	7/80		7/81		+12
7/81		1/82		+6	
	11/82		9/83		+10
Mean				+6	+12
				+9	
Standard deviation				5	6
				7	
Percentage lags				87	100
				94	
Extra cycles		8/51	11/52		
		7/56	6/57		
		6/62	4/63		

CHAPTER 15

A MEASURE OF
UNEMPLOYMENT SEVERITY

Lorene Hiris

The unemployment rate is generally accepted as a measure of the health of the labor market. This rate, however, does not take into account the length of spells of unemployment. During recessions not only are more people unemployed, they tend to be unemployed longer. The unemployment severity index, recently constructed at the CIBCR, takes both factors into account by multiplying the unemployment rate by the average duration of unemployment in weeks.[1] This measures the number of weeks of unemployment per 100 persons in the labor force. For example, the unemployment rate in March 1988 was 5.5 percent and the average unemployed person had been unemployed for 13.7 weeks. The new measure is 5.5 times 13.7, or 75 weeks.

As Chart 15-1 and Table 15-1 show, during recovery periods unemployment severity usually declines (an exception was the brief recovery in 1980–81). During the first 64 months of the current recovery, November 1982 to March 1988, the index dropped from 181 to 75, or by 106 weeks. That is bigger than the total decline during the entire span of any of the previous recoveries. The March level is lower than any level recorded since April 1980.

---

[1] A similar measure was constructed by P. B. Manchester, "A New Measure of Labor Market Distress," *Challenge,* November–December 1982, p. 64. Manchester multiplied the average duration of unemployment by the number of unemployed instead of the unemployment rate. His measure, therefore, tends to rise as the labor force grows.

CHART 15–1
Two Measures of Unemployment

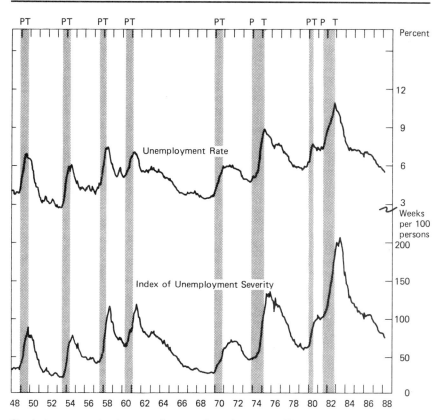

Shaded areas are business cycle recessions, from peak (P) to trough (T).

TABLE 15-1
Unemployment Severity during Business Cycles, 1948–82

Business Cycle Trough Date	Unemployment Severity Index*	Business Cycle Peak Date	Unemployment Severity Index*	Change in Unemployment Severity during Business Cycle	
				Contractions	Expansions
		11/48	29		
10/49	85	7/53	20	56	−65
5/54	66	8/57	42	46	−24
4/58	87	4/60	64	45	−23
2/61	91	12/69	27	27	−64
11/70	53	11/73	48	26	−5
3/75	99	1/80	64	51	−35
7/80	91	7/81	98	27	+7
11/82	181			83	
Average	94		49	45	−30

*Weeks of unemployment per 100 persons in labor force.

The severity index has lagged at nearly all business cycle troughs and has led nearly all the business cycle peaks since 1949 (Table 15-2). In this respect its timing is similar to that of the unemployment rate. However, the lags of the severity index are usually longer at business cycle troughs, whereas its leads at peaks are about the same as those of the unemployment rate.

TABLE 15-2
Leads and Lags of Unemployment Rate and Severity Index

Business Cycle		Unemployment Rate, Inverted		Unemployment Severity Index, Inverted		Lead (−) or Lag (+), in months at Business Cycle Turns			
						Unemployment Rate, Inverted		Severity Index, Inverted	
P	T	P	T	P	T	P	T	P	T
	10/49		10/49		10/49		0		0
7/53	5/54	6/53	9/54	7/53	9/54	−1	+4	0	+4
8/57	4/58	4/57	7/58	3/57	9/58	−4	+3	−5	+5
4/60	2/61	2/60	5/61	5/60	7/61	−2	+3	+1	+5
12/69	11/70	5/69	8/71	5/69	10/71	−7	+9	−7	+11
11/73	3/75	10/73	5/75	9/73	11/75	−1	+2	−2	+8
1/80	7/80	7/79	7/80	7/79	nc	−6	0	−6	ntc
7/81	11/82	7/81	12/82	nc	6/83	0	+1	ntc	+7
Mean						−3	+3	−3	+6
Median						−2	+2	−4	+5

Abbreviations: P, peak; T, trough; ntc, no timing comparison; nc, no cycle.

121

CHAPTER 16

INTERNATIONAL ECONOMIC INDICATORS

Philip A. Klein and Geoffrey H. Moore

In view of the growing importance of international economic relations to the United States, as well as the advances in the statistics available to monitor these relationships, we propose a number of changes in BCD's coverage of this critical area. The changes pertain to two sections in BCD: Section E, U.S. International Transactions, and Section F, International Comparisons, and they are discussed in that order.

U.S. INTERNATIONAL TRANSACTIONS: PRESENT AND PROPOSED COVERAGE

Exports, Imports, and Trade Balance

Chart E1 in BCD shows merchandise exports and imports monthly but only in current dollars, and no trade balance is shown. Chart E2 gives quarterly figures on merchandise trade as well as goods and services from the balance of payments accounts, again only in current dollars and with no trade balance charted separately. Chart A5 in a different section gives goods and services figures quarterly from the national product accounts, in both current and constant dollars and with the net exports balance. We believe that these three sets of figures should be arranged so that they can be compared readily, expressed at annual rates, and stated in constant as well as current dollars and with the surplus or deficit shown in each case.

Also, monthly data on manufactured goods imports and exports should be shown, both in values and quantity indexes.

In addition, consideration should be given to presenting the results of alternative methods of deflating the trade balance. One alternative that is used by the Commerce Department is based solely on import prices. Another method, used by CIBCR, is based on the price deflator for gross domestic purchases. Either of these give a very different picture of the "real" trade surplus or deficit than is shown by the method used in the official GNP statistics, where exports are deflated by export prices and imports by import prices, leaving out the effect on the real balance of shifts in the terms of trade. The official method can change a surplus in current dollars into a deficit in constant dollars, and in fact did so during most of the period from 1958 to 1978 (see Chart 16-1).

Leading Index of U.S. Export Demand

Since the prospects for U.S. exports have become of paramount importance in judging the outlook for the trade balance, consideration should be given to the presentation of leading indexes for other countries in that connection. Analyses at CIBCR have shown that a composite leading index for nine industrial countries other than the United States is a leading indicator of U.S. exports. Growth rates for this index and for exports in constant dollars since 1956 are shown in Chart 16-2. The average lead at peaks and troughs is three months. The correlation is far from perfect, because exports are affected by demand conditions not only in the industrial countries, but also in developing countries and by exchange rates, crop conditions, and so on. Tests have shown that the leading index is especially useful in forecasting exports of manufactured goods. The use in BCD of leading indexes for other countries is discussed later in this Chapter.

Export and Import Prices

Data on export and import price levels and rates of growth should be presented. In addition, the ratio of export to import prices is needed to monitor the terms of trade. The CIBCR has constructed such a measure using the quarterly export and import price deflators from the GNP accounts (see Chart 16-3). For recent years, the BLS fixed-weight export and import price indexes could be used, since they are unaffected by the changing mix of quantities that affect the GNP deflators.

CHART 16–1

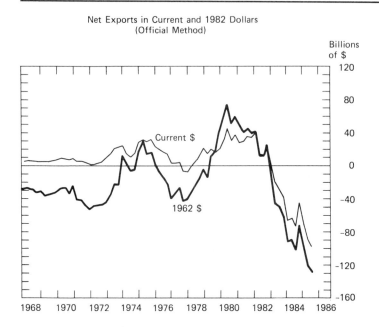

Net Exports in Current and 1982 Dollars
(Official Method)

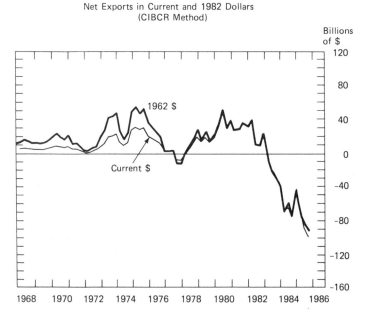

Net Exports in Current and 1982 Dollars
(CIBCR Method)

Source: G. H. Moore, "Needed Improvements in Economic Statistics," *Business Economics,* July 1986, p. 22.

CHART 16-2
Growth Rates in Leading Index of U.S. Export Demand and U.S. Export Volume, 1956-88

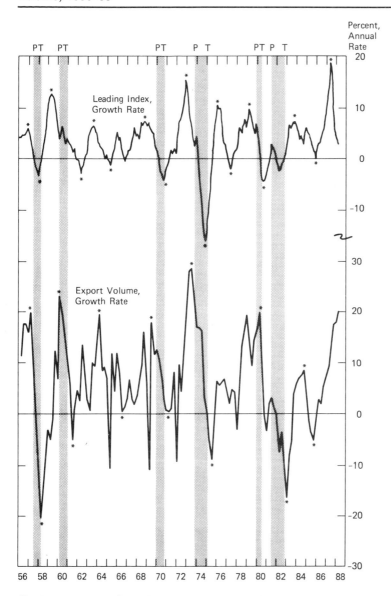

Shaded areas are U.S. business cycle recessions, from peak (P) to trough (T). Leading index is a composite for nine countries: Canada, United Kingdom, West Germany, France, Italy, Japan, Australia, Taiwan, and South Korea. Exports include exports to all countries, in 1982 dollars. Growth rates are six-month smoothed and two-quarter smoothed, respectively, expressed at annual rate.

CHART 16–3
U.S. Terms of Trade Index (Export/Import Prices)

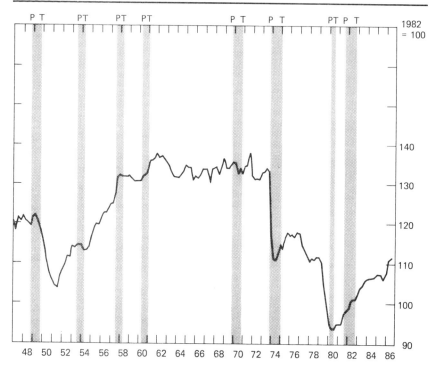

Shaded areas are U.S. business cycle recessions, from peak (P) to trough (T). The price indexes are the implicit price deflators for exports and imports of goods and services, gross national product accounts, U.S. Department of Commerce, quarterly, adjusted for seasonal variations.

Source: Center for International Business Cycle Research, November 1986.

Exchange Rates

In the present era of sporadically managed exchange rates, it is critical to monitor their movements in assessing international economic developments. The data presently included in BCD on an experimental basis in the appendix section should be moved to the regular international section and expanded to include additional multicountry indexes in both real and nominal form. A number of such indexes are now available, including the 27-countries trade-weighted index compiled by the International Monetary Fund (IMF), the Morgan-Guaranty 15- and 44-

countries indexes, and others. Possibly separate indexes should be shown for (1) industrialized countries, (2) developing countries, and (3) non-market–oriented countries.

Foreign Direct Investment

Income from U.S. investment abroad and from foreign investment in the United States is shown in BCD (Chart E2) but not the volume of such investment. Measures of U.S. direct investment abroad and foreign direct investment in the United States should be included in both current and constant dollars.

INTERNATIONAL COMPARISONS: PRESENT AND PROPOSED COVERAGE

The international comparisons in BCD (Charts F1, F2, F3) include series for the United States, Japan, West Germany, France, United Kingdom, Italy, and Canada pertaining to industrial production, consumer prices, and stock prices. We believe that considerably more space, or perhaps a separate publication, should be devoted to this subject. The following items are offered for consideration.

Growth Cycles versus Classical Cycles

We appreciate the fact that BCD has heretofore considered the question of monitoring growth cycles as well as classical business cycles, and it is clearly easier for the public to cope with the material in BCD if it sticks to only one type of cycle chronology. Nevertheless, it must be recognized that most of the major foreign countries are now monitoring only growth cycles, and it is increasingly important to trace developments in various countries on a comparable basis in order to monitor the transmission of economic fluctuations from one country to another. For this purpose, the international comparisons section of BCD could use growth rates and shaded areas based on growth cycle chronologies for each country. The CIBCR currently has such chronologies for 15 countries including, of course, all the countries now represented in BCD.[1]

---

[1]See P. A. Klein and G. H. Moore, *Monitoring Growth Cycles in Market-Oriented Countries,* Ballinger Publishing Co. for the National Bureau of Economic Research, Cambridge, MA, 1985.

CHART 16–4
Growth Rates in Leading and Coincident Indexes, 10 Countries, 1976–86

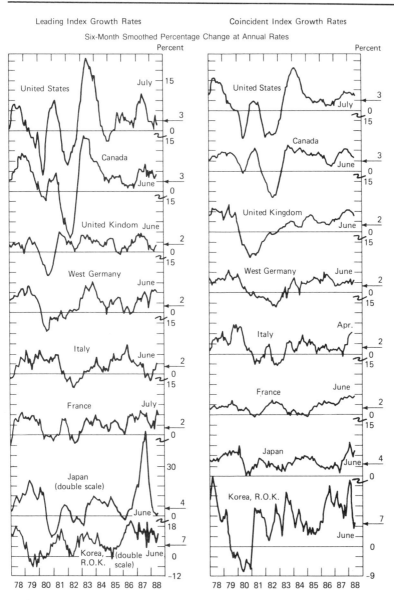

Leading Index Growth Rates   Coincident Index Growth Rates

Six-Month Smoothed Percentage Change at Annual Rates

Arrows indicate rate of change, 1976–86, in the index and real gross national product.

Source: Center for International Business Cycle Research and the Conference Board.

CHART 16–4—*Continued*

Leading Index Growth Rates

Coincident Index Growth Rates

Six-Month Smoothed Percentage Change at Annual Rates

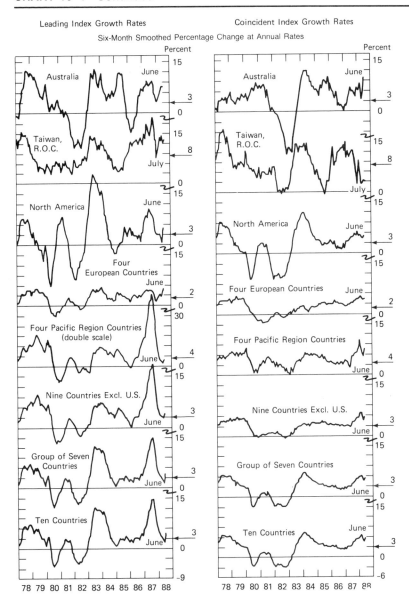

Arrows indicate rate of change, 1976–86, in the index and real gross national product.

Source: Center for International Business Cycle Research and the Conference Board.

Real GNP

It would be desirable to include quarterly figures for real GNP, which are now available for many countries. The rapid growth in the service sector in most countries makes industrial production alone increasingly inadequate as the sole output variable being tracked. Growth rates in real GNP should be shown.

Unemployment Rates

Because of their wide interest and importance, a set of comparable unemployment rates for the major industrialized countries should be included. The BLS compiles such data monthly for eight countries.

Composite Leading and Coincident Indexes

The preeminent feature that distinguishes BCD is, of course, the U.S. leading, coincident, and lagging indexes. In recent years such indexes have been constructed by a number of individual countries as well as by the Organization for Economic Cooperation and Development and by the CIBCR. The Klein/Moore book referred to in the preceding footnote examines the historical behavior of composite indexes for 10 market-oriented countries since the 1950s. These indexes are kept up to date and are comparable across countries in both content and method in so far as possible. The growth rates in these indexes expose the cyclical movements clearly and could be used for graphic presentation (see Chart 16-4).

The CIBCR has also developed such indexes for groups of countries, such as the G-7 group. The growth rate in the leading index covering nine countries excluding the United States has been found to be a useful leading indicator of U.S. exports as noted above.

Business Outlook Surveys

Surveys of business enterprises actual and expected changes in sales, employment, inventories, prices, and so on are widely used in many countries as very promptly available indicators. The inclusion of summary data from these surveys would improve the timeliness of the international coverage.

Surveys of Economic Forecasts

A survey of professional economic forecasts for 10 individual countries has been compiled monthly since 1981 by Blue Chip Economic Worldscan. It covers real GNP, industrial production, consumer prices, and the current account balance. Since we have proposed to include in BCD several consensus forecast surveys for the United States, some coverage of this sort might be included also for other countries. Measures of the past accuracy of the forecasts could be shown, using results of analyses made at CIBCR.

CHAPTER 17

SOURCES AND DESCRIPTIONS OF NEW INDICATORS RECOMMENDED BY CIBCR

Melita H. Moore

List of Indicators (see Chapter 1)

Long Leading
 1. Corporate bond prices.
 2. Ratio, price to unit labor cost, manufacturing.

Short Leading
 3. Net change in business population.
 4. Layoff rate.
 5. Inventory change survey.
 6. Vendor performance survey.
 7. Industrial materials price index, growth rate.
 8. Domestic nonfinancial debt, deflated, growth rate.

Coincident
 9. Employee-hours in nonagricultural establishments.
 10. Consumer goods and capital goods sales.

Lagging
 11. Unit labor cost, manufacturing, growth rate.
 12. Consumer price index, services, growth rate.

1. CORPORATE BOND PRICES

Monthly, beginning 1947.

Unit: Percentage of the face value of the bonds represented as 100.

Title in Source: Dow Jones Bond Averages.

Source: *Wall Street Journal.*

Description: This series is the Dow Jones Bond Averages for 20 corporate bonds listed on the New York Exchange. The figures, published daily, are an unweighted average of the closing prices of 10 public utilities and 10 industrial bonds. Prior to July 1976, 20 railroad bond issues were also included. The sample of corporate issues is changed from time to time as issues near maturity or because of other factors that might distort the price of a particular issue. The series is not seasonally adjusted.

The monthly averages for the preceding month of this daily series are published in the first weekly issue of *Barron's* in each month.

2. RATIO, PRICE TO UNIT LABOR COST, MANUFACTURING

Monthly, beginning 1979; quarterly, 1947–78.

Unit: Index, base 1982 = 100.

Titles in Sources: Price series: Producer price index for net output, manufacturing. Unit labor cost: Total labor compensation in manufacturing, divided by gross domestic product in manufacturing in constant prices.

Sources: Price series from *Producer Price Indexes,* monthly release of the BLS; labor compensation data from BLS and the BEA; gross domestic product in manufacturing in constant prices from the July issue of *Survey of Current Business,* Department of Commerce.

Description: The monthly price series beginning in 1979 is a producer price index for net output in manufacturing, seasonally adjusted by the CIBCR. The net output (or value added) weights avoid double counting of sales by some manufacturing industries to others. The monthly price index was estimated by CIBCR from 1979 to 1985, then linked to the published BLS index in December 1984. The quarterly price series, 1947–78, is the annual implicit price deflator for gross domestic product in manufacturing (from the Department of Commerce National Income and Product Accounts, published in the July issue of *Survey of Current Business*), interpolated by CIBCR on the basis of quarterly movements of the implicit price deflator for gross domestic product, nonfarm business. The latter series, seasonally adjusted by the BLS, is published in its quarterly release, *Productivity and Costs.*

The unit labor cost series, available monthly from 1947, is computed by CIBCR. It is the ratio of total compensation (wages, salaries, and supplements) in manufacturing to total real domestic product in manufacturing. The compensation series is compiled by BEA from BLS data. The output series is based on annual data on real domestic product originating in manufacturing from the National Income and Product Accounts of the BEA, interpolated monthly by CIBCR, using the index of manufacturing production of the FRB. Both series are seasonally adjusted by the source agencies. The monthly unit labor cost series is equivalent to the quarterly unit labor cost index in manufacturing, base 1977=100, published by the BLS in its quarterly release, *Productivity and Costs.*

3. NET CHANGE IN BUSINESS POPULATION

Monthly, beginning 1948.

Unit: Index, base 1980 = 100.

Titles in Sources: Number of business starts; number of business failures.

Source: *Weekly Business Starts* and *Weekly Business Failures,* Dun & Bradstreet Corporation. Seasonally adjusted by CIBCR.

Description: This series provides an estimate of the net formation of business enterprises. There are no direct measures of the monthly change in the total population, but it is believed that these estimates adequately represent the short-term movement of new entries into and departures from the business population. The index has two components, both supplied by the Dun & Bradstreet Corporation: one is the number of new business starts; the other, the number of business failures. Because business failures do not cover all types of discontinuances and, hence, are not commensurate with business starts, the basic data cannot be subtracted. Rather, each series is treated as a component of a composite index with changes in failures taken inversely. The index is constructed according to the method used by the Department of Commerce in its leading index except that no adjustment is made in the long-run trend of the index.

The series on business starts consists of newly opened active establishments. It does not include changes in ownership of previously operating businesses or changes in the name, location, legal type, or mergers. All industries in the United States are presented. A business start is included in the current year if the birth date is within the last 36 months.

About 56 percent of the business starts in 1986 employed one or two people. Firms employing three to five workers represented 24 percent of starts and companies with 6 to 10 workers contributed 11 percent of the total. Businesses with more than 10 employees represented about 9 percent of all starts.

Because the series for business starts began only in 1985, it has been linked to the Dun & Bradstreet series for new business incorporations covering the number of stock companies receiving charters each month. Figures prior to 1958 do not include Hawaii, those prior to 1960 do not include Alaska, and those prior to 1963 do not include the District of Columbia. The figures include new businesses that are incorporated, existing businesses that are changed from a noncorporate to a corporate form of organization, existing corporations that have been given certificates of authority to operate also in another state, and existing corporations transferred to a new state. Data are collected from the secretaries of state for each state government.

Dun & Bradstreet has for many years compiled the weekly number of business failures. A business failure is defined as a concern that is involved in a court proceeding or a voluntary action that is likely to result in loss to creditors. Firms that are liquidated, merged, sold, or otherwise discontinued without loss to creditors are not considered failures. The data cover the 50 states and the District of Columbia. At the beginning of 1984 the coverage of the failures series was extended to cover additional industries.

4. LAYOFF RATE

Monthly, beginning 1948.

Unit: Percentage.

Title in Source: Job losers on layoff, under five weeks, divided by total civilian employment; 1948–68, layoff rate, manufacturing.

Source: Employment & Earnings, U.S. Department of Labor, BLS, seasonally adjusted by CIBCR. 1948–68 data also published in BCD (series 3), Department of Commerce.

Description: The layoff rate under five weeks has been derived by the CIBCR from data published by the BLS concerning the household survey of unemployment. The survey is conducted each month by interviewers of the U.S. Department of Commerce, Bureau of the Census, as part of the current population survey. The layoff rate is the ratio of the number of unemployed persons who were laid off within the past five weeks to total civilian employment. Job losers on layoff are classified by the length of time they have been unemployed. Those in the shortest class, under five weeks, evidently correspond closely to those included in reports by employers on the number of employees laid off during the past month.

The 1948–68 data are a component of the BLS series on labor turnover in manufacturing establishments, which were discontinued after December 1981. Data were collected from employers by state employment security agencies. Each agency used the information to develop turnover rates for the state and its metropolitan areas and forwarded the data to the BLS, which prepared rates at the national level. During the period 1969–81, the layoff rate from the household survey corresponds closely in its major movements to the layoff rate in manufacturing, although the household survey series is not limited to manufacturing and is subject to a larger sampling error. In December 1981, the layoffs in manufacturing were about 52 percent of total layoffs in the household survey.

5. INVENTORY CHANGE SURVEY

Monthly, beginning 1948.

Unit: Percentage rising.

Title in Source: Inventories.

Source: Report on Business, NAPM, seasonally adjusted by CIBCR.

Description: Data are derived from a survey by the Business Survey Committee of the NAPM. The committee comprises 250 members (soon to be extended to 300 members) selected from the approximately 30,000 NAPM membership. The Survey Committee members must have purchasing responsibility for a manufacturing company identified by one of the SIC numbers (SIC #20–#39). Membership is diversified according to (1) SIC category, based on each industry's contribution to national income, and (2) geographic location, based on value added by state. Each member must be actively involved in the purchasing function within a manufacturing company, typically the vice-president, director or manager of purchasing or materials management. Members are encouraged to train a subordinate to respond to the monthly questionnaire whenever they are not able to do so. No responses are considered valid unless they are from the committee member or the duly authorized substitute.

Members provide information on whether their inventories have increased, decreased, or stayed the same. The index figure represents the percentage of the total of those whose inventories have increased plus one-half of those whose inventories have stayed the same (diffusion index). The index is unweighted. Typical monthly responses run in excess of 80 percent of the total sample and calculation of the results is delayed until a minimum of two-thirds of the sample has been received.

6. VENDOR PERFORMANCE SURVEY

Monthly, beginning 1948.

Unit: Percentage of companies receiving slower deliveries.

Title in Source: Vendor deliveries.

Source: *Report on Business*, NAPM, seasonally adjusted by CIBCR.

Description: Data are derived from the survey by the Business Survey Committee of the NAPM described in the inventory change. Each month, committee members are asked to report whether deliveries are faster than last month, the same, or slower than last month. A figure is computed by summing up the percentage receiving slower deliveries plus one-half of the percentage receiving deliveries unchanged from the previous month. This reflects the volume of business being handled by the supplier firms, with slower deliveries usually indicating a higher volume of business. The series also reflects the ratio of inventories to sales, because low inventories usually means slower deliveries.

Prior to 1969, the data relate to vendor performance in the greater Chicago area only, since the NAPM series is not available before 1969. This survey is conducted monthly among 200 of the approximately 1,000 members of the Purchasing Management Association of Chicago. The sample is selected to represent proportionally 15 industries in the greater Chicago area. Figures are published as series 32 in BCD.

7. INDUSTRIAL MATERIALS PRICE INDEX, GROWTH RATE

Monthly, beginning 1948.

Unit: Percentages, annual rate.

Title in Source: *The Journal of Commerce* daily industrial materials price index of sensitive spot commodity prices.

Source: *The Journal of Commerce,* not seasonally adjusted.

Description: This index, designed by CIBCR, includes the prices of 18 important materials used in manufacturing, energy production, and building construction and is published daily. The commodities are close to the initial stages of production whose markets are presumed to be among the first to be influenced by changes in economic conditions. The items covered are: cotton, burlap, printcloth, polyester, steel scrap, copper scrap, lead, zinc, tin, aluminum, hides, rubber, tallow, plywood, red oak, old corrugated boxes, benzene, and crude petroleum. Subgroup indexes covering textiles, metals, and miscellaneous, are published.

The method used in computing the index is a slightly modified version of the composite index methodology used by the Department of Commerce in the leading index of business cycles. Items are weighted on the basis of their economic significance and their performance as leading indicators of inflation.

The rate of change computed by the CIBCR is a 6-month smoothed annual rate, based upon the ratio of the current month's index to the average index of the preceding 12 months. Because the interval between midpoints of the current month and the preceding 12 is 6.5 months, the ratio is raised to the 12/6.5 power to derive a compound annual rate. A similar rate is published daily, based on the ratio of the current day's index to the average index for the preceding 250 working days, the approximate number in a calendar year. This ratio is squared to derive a compound annual rate.

8. DOMESTIC NONFINANCIAL DEBT, DEFLATED, GROWTH RATE

Monthly, beginning January 1955.

Unit: Percentage change at annual rate.

Title in Source: Total net borrowing by domestic nonfinancial sectors.

Sources: *Federal Reserve Bulletin* and *Money Stock, Liquid Assets and Debt Measures,* Statistical Release H6, Board of Governors of the Federal Reserve System; seasonal adjustment by source.

Description: The basic data in billions of dollars are shown in the source by the two main sectors: U.S. government borrowing (Treasury securities and agency issues and mortgages) and the private domestic nonfinancial sector. The private sector includes debt capital instruments (tax-exempt obligations, corporate bonds, and mortgages) and other debt instruments (consumer credit, bank loans, open market paper, and others). The private nonfinancial sector data are also presented by borrowing sector: state and local governments, households, farms, nonfarm noncorporate, and corporate.

The CIBCR deflates the debt by the CPI and computes the 6-month smoothed percentage change from the deflated figures. The 6-month smoothed annual rate is based upon the ratio of the current month's debt to the average debt over the preceding 12 months. Because the interval between midpoints of the current month and the preceding 12 is 6.5 months, the ratio is raised to the 12/6.5 power to derive a compound annual rate.

9. EMPLOYEE–HOURS IN NONAGRICULTURAL ESTABLISHMENTS

Monthly, beginning 1948.

Unit: Billion employee hours, annual rate.

Title in Source: Employee hours in nonagricultural establishments.

Sources: *Employment and Earnings,* BLS, and BCD (series 48), Department of Commerce; seasonally adjusted by BLS.

Description: Data are obtained principally from the establishment survey conducted each month by the BLS. The number of hours worked are derived primarily from payroll records voluntarily reported each month by employers to state employment security agencies in the 50 states and the District of Columbia. Data relate to the payroll period that includes the 12th of the month (end-of-month data for federal government employees). Total hours paid for one week in the month, seasonally adjusted, are multiplied by 52.

Data refer to hours of production workers, nonsupervisory workers, and salaried workers. They include full-time, part-time, temporary, and permanent workers. Persons on paid leave and those who worked only during part of the pay period are included. Persons on the payroll of more than one establishment are counted each time they are reported, so their total hours are recorded. Excluded are: persons on a nonpay status for the entire period due to layoff, strike, or leave without pay; the self-employed, unpaid volunteer, and family workers; farm and domestic workers; and noncivilian government employees.

The industries included (and reported separately) are mining; construction; manufacturing; transportation and public utilities; wholesale trade; retail trade; finance, insurance, and real estate; services; and government.

Hours worked are computed separately for each industry and aggregated into the nonfarm total. Where data are lacking for individual industries, other sources are used—primarily the Current Population Survey for weekly hours, adjusted to eliminate distortions due to holidays. Methods of imputation to supply missing data for various sectors are outlined in some detail in the U.S. Department of Commerce, Bureau of Economic Analysis, *Handbook of Cyclical Indicators,* 1984, p. 6.

As a measure of labor input, this series is superior to the number of employees on payrolls, mainly because it reflects the declines in the average workweek during recessions. Moreover, the payroll employment series counts part-time and full-time employees alike and, hence, rises faster than total hours when the proportion working part-time increases. The payroll employment series also double counts persons with more than one job.

There are two deficiencies in the hours series as published: erratic movements in the series when holidays occur during the survey week (the BLS is undertaking to remedy this) and publication lag between the data for employee-hours of production workers and those for all employees. To provide up-to-date figures, the CIBCR estimates nonproduction worker hours by multiplying the previous month's average workweek of nonproduction workers by the current month's number employed.

10. CONSUMER GOODS AND CAPITAL GOODS SALES (IN CONSTANT PRICES)

Monthly, beginning 1948.

Unit: Millions of 1982 dollars.

Titles in Source: (1) Retail trade sales in 1982 dollars. (2) Shipments of capital goods industries in 1982 dollars.

Source: Survey of Current Business, Department of Commerce series seasonally adjusted in the source.

Description: The retail sales component of this series measures the net sales and receipts of establishments primarily engaged in retail trade. Wholesale sales of retail establishments are included, but retail sales of manufacturing, wholesale, service, and other establishments whose primary activity is not retail trade are excluded.

Net sales are defined as cash and credit sales less discounts, refunds, and allowances for returned merchandise but without deductions for trade-in allowances. Since 1967, finance charges and sales and excise taxes collected from customers and paid directly to tax agencies are excluded.

Since 1951, sales of retail stores are estimated by the Bureau of the Census from data reported in its monthly survey of retail establishments. Estimates are prepared from probability sample data stratified by industry, size, and geographic location. They are derived by weighting the reported sales of each store in the sample by a value inversely proportionate to its probability of selection. Data are adjusted to the levels reported in the census of retail trade collected in selected years and to the annual survey of retail trade. For 1947–50, the BEA prepared a series that is similar to the Census Bureau series.

The series in 1982 dollars is computed by the BEA by deflating the current dollar series by sub-indexes of CPI compiled by the BLS.

The capital goods component of this series since 1958 measures shipments of capital goods industries (defense and nondefense), including manufacturers' receipts or the value of products shipped, less discounts, returns, and allowances, and excluding freight charges and excise taxes. Shipments for export as well as for domestic use are included. Shipments by foreign subsidiaries are excluded, but shipments by a domestic firm to a foreign subsidiary are included. Figures are benchmarked to an annual survey of manufacturers and include interplant transfers as well as commercial sales. This is a sample survey of approximately 56,000 manufacturing establishments.

The monthly estimates are based on information obtained from most manufacturing companies with 1,000 or more employees (some smaller companies are included in individual industry categories). Figures are derived for each industry category by multiplying the industry estimate for the previous month by the percentage change from the previous month for companies reporting in the current month. Data are adjusted for trading day and calendar month variations and are seasonally adjusted.

Capital goods shipments are published separately for nondefense and defense industries. Nondefense industries include machinery and electrical machinery (but excluding farm machinery, household appliances, radio and television, and electronic components); railroad equipment; and the nondefense portions of shipbuilding and military tank vehicles, communications equipment, aircraft and aircraft parts, and ordnance. Defense products are based on separate reports on defense work filed by large defense contractors in the following industries: ordnance, communication equipment, complete aircraft and aircraft parts, shipbuilding, and military tank vehicles. This series is comparable to data published prior to 1972 in the categories "producers' capital goods" and "defense products" (old series).

Capital goods shipments in 1982 dollars are calculated by the BEA by deflating the current dollar series with producer price indexes.

Because shipments data are not available prior to 1958, the earlier figures are derived from the index of industrial production, business equipment including defense, issued by the Board of Governors of the Federal Reserve System, Division of Research and Statistics. The CIBCR multiplied the index figures (1977 = 100) by the ratio of the monthly average of capital goods shipments in millions of 1982 dollars during 1958 to the monthly average of this production index during 1958. The ratio is 11,863/43.1 = 275.25.

11. UNIT LABOR COST, MANUFACTURING, GROWTH RATE

Monthly, beginning 1948.

Unit: Percentage, at annual rate.

Titles in Sources: Total labor compensation in manufacturing divided by gross domestic product in manufacturing in constant prices.

Sources: Labor compensation data from the BLS and the BEA; gross domestic product in manufacturing in constant prices from the *Survey of Current Business*, BEA, Department of Commerce. Monthly data are adjusted by CIBCR to levels of the quarterly unit labor cost series in manufacturing from the BLS quarterly release *Productivity and Costs*.

Description: This is the same unit labor cost series in manufacturing described above in Series 2, Ratio, Price to Unit Labor Cost, Manufacturing. It is computed by CIBCR and is the ratio of total compensation (wages, salaries, and supplements) in manufacturing to total real domestic product in manufacturing. The compensation series is compiled by BEA from BLS data. The output series is based on annual data from the National Income and Product Accounts of the BEA, interpolated monthly by CIBCR, using the index of manufacturing production of the FRB. The monthly unit labor cost calculated in this way corresponds closely to the quarterly unit labor cost in manufacturing, base 1977 = 100, published by BLS. Data are seasonally adjusted in the sources.

The rate of change in monthly unit labor cost is a 6-month smoothed annual rate, based upon the ratio of the current month's index to the average index for the preceding 12 months. Because the interval between midpoints of the current month and the preceding 12 is 6.5 months, the ratio is raised to the 12/6.5 power to derive a compound annual rate.

12. CONSUMER PRICE INDEX, SERVICES, GROWTH RATE

Monthly beginning 1957.

Unit: Percentage at annual rate.

Title in Source: Consumer price index for all urban consumers (CPI-U): services.

Source: CPI Detailed Report, BLS; seasonally adjusted by BLS.

Description: The CPI-U represents about 80 percent of the total noninstitutional population of the United States, including all consumer units in urban areas with two exceptions: those living on farms in urban areas and those receiving a majority of their income from a member in the Armed Forces, but living within the consumer unit. Currently the CPI-U is based upon weights derived from a Consumer Expenditure Survey carried out in 1982–84 with information from about 4,800 families. The index is published on the base 1982–84 = 100. Prices are collected from more than 21,000 retail establishments and 60,000 housing units in 91 urban areas across the country. The price index for services is available only from 1956 and constituted about 54 percent of the total CPI-U in December 1987.

The price index for services is composed of the following components:

Category	*Relative Importance, December 1987 (%)*
1. Rent of shelter	27.151
2. Household services less rent of shelter	9.359
3. Transportation services	6.646
4. Medical care services	4.715
5. Other services	6.599
Total services	54.469

1. Includes not only rent paid by renters but also the equivalent rent of owner-occupied homes, reflecting a flow-of-services concept of owner housing rather than the investment concept.
2. Includes housekeeping services, insurance, gas and electricity, and other utilities and public services.
3. Includes auto maintenance, repairs and insurance, other private transportation services, and public transportation.

4. Includes professional services, hospital services, and outpatient services.
5. Includes apparel services, entertainment, personal and educational services, and personal care.

The rate of change computed by CIBCR is a 6-month smoothed annual rate, based upon the ratio of the current month's seasonally adjusted index to the average index of the preceding 12 months. Because the interval between midpoints of the current month and the preceding 12 is 6.5 months, the ratio is raised to the 12/6.5 power to derive a compound annual rate.

INDEX